DORSET'S MOST BEAUTIFUL BUILDINGS

For Rosemary and Ashlynne who were left to their own devices on the best days of the last two years.

DORSET'S
MOST BEAUTIFUL BUILDINGS

By ROGER HOLMAN

with descriptive text by **BILL HOADE**

DORSET BOOKS

First published in 2001 by Dorset Books
Text © 2001 Bill Hoade
Images © 2001 Roger Holman

ISBN 1 871164 80 X

British Library Cataloguing-in-Publication-Data
A CIP data record for this book is available from the British Library

DORSET BOOKS
Offical Publisher to Dorset County Council
Halsgrove House
Lower Moor Way
Tiverton EX16 6SS
T: 01884 243242
F: 01884 243325
www.halsgrove.com

Printed and bound in Italy
by Centro Grafico Ambrosiano

CONTENTS

THE COUNTY OF
DORSET

SANDFORD ORCAS

TRENT

SHERBORNE
OVER COMPTON

PURSE CAUNDLE

HAMOON
IWERNE MINSTER

RANSTON
HANFORD
CHETTLE

PULHAM
TARRANT
HINTON
WIMBORNE ST GILES

EDMONDSHAM

FORDE ABBEY
HOLDITCH COURT

RAMPISHAM

BUCKLAND NEWTON
PLUSH

BLANDFORD FORUM

WOODLANDS
HORTON

CHALMINGTON
CHANTMARLE

CERNE ABBAS

WINTEBORNE
CLENSTON
SPETISBURY

STANBRIDGE

BEAMINSTER

MILTON ABBAS

PARNHAM
MAPPERTON
MELPLASH

MAIDEN NEWTON

WINTERBORNE
WHITECHURCH
KINGSTON LACY
PAMPHILL

MONKTON WYLD

ANDERSON
WINTERBORNE
THOMSON
WIMBORNE MINSTER

LYME REGIS
CHIDEOCK

BRIDPORT

FRAMPTON

COMPTON
VALANCE

WATERSTON

PUDDLETOWN
CHARMINSTER
ATHELHAMPTON

TINCLETON

CHRISTCHURCH
HIGHCLIFFE

LITTLE BREDY

DORCHESTER
POOLE

PUNCKNOWLE

WOODSFORD

BOURNEMOUTH
WESTBOURNE

CAME HOUSE

WOOL

ABBOTSBURY
WARMWELL
OWERMOIGNE

BINDON
ABBEY
WAREHAM

OSMINGTON

CREECH
GRANGE
BARNSTON
CORFE
CASTLE
STUDLAND

LULWORTH

KINGSTON
AFFLINGTON
GODLINGSTON

WEYMOUTH

SMEDMORE

ENCOMBE

PORTLAND

ST ALDHEIM'S HEAD

BOW & ARROW CASTLE

MEDIEVAL ARCHITECTURE

From Castle to Manor – 1066–1400

The necessity for solid defensive structures (partly for the safety of the inhabitants and to show a physical military presence to those peoples who have been conquered) means that castles are some of the earliest masonry buildings to survive.

The Anglo-Saxons, as far as we know, had no stone defensive structures or domestic buildings and only in the building of their churches do we find the use of this material. One possible exception may be a section of wall incorporated in the original hall of Corfe Castle.

Fortified Burhs, such as **Wareham**, consisted of a square earthen rampart with a wooden stockade to protect their dwellings; the Saxon church of **St Martin** stands on these ramparts.

The Norman conquest of Britain wrought great changes. Not the least of the problems was that of language; the Saxons, themselves conquerors, spoke the first forms of the English language, while the Normans spoke French. Latin was the accepted language of the church and the learned classes. The conquerors provided us with many generations of French Kings and French nobility and it

Wareham: St. Martin.

was some five hundred years before the English language (that we now recognize) was fully formed with its borrowings and corruptions from French, Latin and other sources. An inability to communicate with the people of the time, and more especially with the artisan class, coupled with the natural resentment of the subjugated populace, meant that for many years Norman masons were imported to oversee any construction work and 'English' Norman architecture was stylistically based on the French Romanesque.

King William took some time to subdue the Saxon population and embarked on a scheme of fortress building, initially import-ing Caen Stone from his native Normandy but in time quarrying and using indigenous stone. In the period of just over a single century between the conquest and the end of the reign of Henry II (1189), over 1000 castles had been built in England and Wales.

The earliest of these castles followed the Saxon example but with French innovations and improvements. The form usually adopted was the motte and bailey, which consisted of a circular mound with a wooden keep and a lower bailey (or court) usually of circular form, with an earthen rampart and a wooden stockade. These had the advantage of quick construction and in the fullness of time could be strengthened with stone constructions where necessary.

The finest example of a motte and bailey castle of the earliest and simplest type in Dorset, is to be found at Cranborne where the Victorian penchant for planting trees on conspicuous earthworks has all but obscured it. Others are known to have existed at Marshwood (where there are the remains of a keep and clear evidence of a moat), Powerstock, Dorchester, Lulworth, Sturminster Newton and Wareham; parts of Sherborne Old Castle, Shaftesbury; and possibly parts of the foundations of the pentagonal tower of **Bow and Arrow Castle (Rufus castle)** at Portland *(40)*. This, according to Derek Renn, '... *may have been a twelfth century keep'*. Hutchins states that it was called Rufus castle because, '*It is supposed to have been built by William Rufus...*' However, J. H. Bettey has made the suggestion that 'Rufus' may have been an allusion to Robert, Earl of Gloucester, also known as Rufus or the Red Earl, who in 1142 captured the castle from King Stephen for the Empress Matilda. Permission to crenellate was granted in 1258 but Richard, Duke of York, built the extant remains between 1432 and 1460.

The county boundary changes of 1974 have meant that the town of **Christchurch**, along with its magnificent **priory** and castle ruins *(41)* which date from the late twelfth century, are now firmly placed within the county of Dorset. But the most important monument of Norman achievement within the county must be the nucleus of the stone built castle of **Corfe** *(42)*.

King William I began the building of the stone castle here before the year 1086 (Hutchins). Earlier occupation of the hill as a defensive site is uncertain although the inference has been made that a Saxon castle may have existed here, as King Edward the Martyr was, according to the Anglo-Saxon Chronicle, assassinated at 'Corfesgeate' in 978. However, this name merely describes the gap in the Purbeck Hills. The Anglo-Saxon Chronicle makes no mention of a castle here and with the Saxon fortified town of Wareham nearby, the likelihood is that a royal house was built here and that the herringbone masonry in the south wall of the 'hall' in the west bailey is the only remnant of that building, dressed by the Norman masons with ashlar and pierced by three round-headed Norman windows. Most of the enceinte wall of the inner ward and the tower keep are from the earliest Norman period.

Corfe Castle is built on a natural hill, but the keep at Christchurch was erected on the artificial mound of a simple motte and bailey castle which had in its turn replaced the Saxon fortifications, all traces of which are now lost beneath the Saxon Square car park and modern buildings. The Saxon defences of Thuinam (or Twynham, as the town is recorded in the Domesday book) were primarily used as a safe haven from Viking raiders and the new motte and bailey castle was built as a show of Norman strength. On coming to the throne, Henry I gave Richard de Redvers, the Earl of Devon and a distant relation to the conqueror, the manor of Christchurch and he added the masonry keep and curtain walls to the castle of the growing town.

Richard died in 1137 and his grandson, also named Richard, succeeded him. In 1150, he granted Christchurch its first charter. He was also responsible for the most interesting and important

Christchurch: the Constable's House.

building here, the hall, which stands in the curtain wall of the bailey, erected some ten or twelve years later. This house measures only 70 feet by 20 feet and consists of a ground floor over an undercroft or cellar, this latter providing a safe storage area and raising the first floor to a defensible height above the ground. No expense was spared here. Whereas the main construction of the castle was built with stone quarried on the Isle of Wight, the **Constable's House** (as the hall was later known) is built of rough blocks of Purbeck marble, an unusual (and doubtless expensive) choice of material, of which we will learn more when we consider the manor houses and quarries of Purbeck. Simple oblong loopholes lighted the ground floor windows with wide internal splays both in their heads and jambs to maximize the shaft of light that entered. The first floor has two-light widows with a single shaft or mullion (of polished Purbeck marble) but, remarkable as this building is for the stone of its construction, it contains another architectural gem, the first floor fireplace being one of the few remaining examples of an early Norman fireplace with a flue and circular chimneystack. In addition to being the hall of the castle the building was used by the Constable, whose role was chief officer or administrator of all military affairs relating to the castle and town and for this reason the building is better known to this day as the Constable's House.

The Growth Of Domestic Architecture

European architecture of the next three centuries reflects the need for security; the materials used in the construction of many settlement and village buildings was wood, with wattle and daub for the walls and roofs normally thatched with reeds or straw. Very few of these have survived so their form is known only from archaeological excavation and scant written descriptions. Of the stone defensible buildings a few have survived, mostly concealed in later rebuilding and alterations. The sanctuary provided by the solid stone castles and fortified manor houses declined with the greater employment of canon and gunpowder in the late fourteenth century.

Dorset has two examples of thirteenth century domestic architecture, the earliest being the remains of King John's hunting lodge incorporated into the Jacobean Manor House at Cranborne. The original lodge dates from 1207–8 and the extant remains consist of a rectangular building with a first floor chapel, which stood on an undercroft (crypt) and a defensive tower at the south-west corner.

The second is the magnificent **Moigne Court** at Owermoigne *(43)*, a first floor hall and solar block with a north-south orientation built to a similar design as the castle hall at Christchurch, but here in its original form (with the possible addition of a solar on the east side). The present east wing is unfortunately modern as is the cross-wing to the south. A drawing dated October 1876 entitled *The 'Court House', Ower Moigne, Dorsetshire* in the Dorset collection, shows the eastern elevation and the extent of the original building without the modern additions, the building thatched and with an entrance between the two chimneybreasts.

Swanage: Godlingston Manor.

The three magnificent bar-traceried windows that light the first floor hall are an amazing survival. The central of these may have been moved from its original position in the gable of the north wall and reset here in the nineteenth century and the external buttress-like projection beneath this window may have supported a first floor fireplace, the removal of which would have facilitated the insertion of the window, but for this sadly there is no evidence. The tracery of the windows is fashioned from Ham Hill stone and the heads and jambs are of Purbeck stone. Of the ground floor windows with their stone mullions and transoms, the southernmost dates from the sixteenth century and the others from the nineteenth. Entrance to the first floor hall was by way of an external staircase on the east side where there is a blocked doorway with mouldings similar to the windows and with a date of c.1270. The site was never fortified but moated for defence and the shape of the moat can still be seen easily despite being filled in to the west of the building in the late nineteenth century to make a croquet lawn.

Godlingston Manor north of Swanage, has a low D-shaped tower at its western end. The present building is of the seventeenth and eighteenth centuries on thirteenth century foundations; the only extant thirteenth century feature being the doorway in the south wall, which with its chamfered and tre-foiled two-centred head and continuous jambs is one of the most beautiful survivals in the county. That it has survived in such a good state is amazing when one considers the many changes and indignities that the building (in common with other Purbeck houses) has suffered. The original rectangular building with its tower was remodelled first in the seventeenth century with the rebuilding of the north wall and the addition of a stair turret to the upper rooms built above the hall. In the eighteenth century a kitchen wing was added to the north which itself was altered and extended later in that same century and at some stage a cross wing was added to the east. In 1867 Thomas Bond wrote '…*these interesting remains have been permitted to fall into a sad state of dilapidation, and it is now contemplated to sweep them all away, to make room for a brand new farm-house…*' adding, '*Such destruction will be deplored by everyone who has any regard for mediaeval architecture, or even for what is merely picturesque.*' A fire in 1871 destroyed the east wing and many of the farm buildings but thankfully the building was rescued and again rebuilt with the addition of the present east wing and the internal remodelling of the remaining medieval features.

Godlingston is now generally accepted as the home of Durand, carpenter to William the Conqueror. He is named in the Domesday book as the owner of the tenement of "Moulham" which he held in return for his work at the castle of Corfe, and he is also recorded therein as holding land at Wilkswood and Afflington. In the late eleventh and early twelfth century, a group of substantial houses was built along what is now referred to as the marble line which is within the upper Purbeck beds that run diagonally across the island from Peveril Point westwards to Worbarrow Tout.

These beds contained Purbeck marble, which was first mined and used by the Romans for loom weights, tombstones and at Silchester in Hampshire as one of the stones for the mosaic floor of the church. In the late eleventh century interest blossomed again and the marble became highly prized as a decorative stone, capable of taking a high polish and it was used extensively for fonts, collonettes and other architectural features. Over the next century it flowered into one of the most lucrative mediaeval businesses when alongside of the existing usage, the fashion for sculptured tomb effigies grew. This demand continued to grow until the beginning of the fourteenth century when the rising price of the raw material (which was becoming difficult to procure in pieces large enough for effigies) and the desire for more elaborate carvings which were more easily fashioned out of wood, stone or alabaster (which materials could better take the application of colour) would seem to have virtually closed down the quarries, the tumbled remains of which can still be seen.

The changing fortunes and subsequent migrations of the work force greatly affected the buildings associated with the marble and stone industries. The nature and rough dating of these changes can be deduced from examination of the renovations and rebuilding of two of them, the manor houses of **Afflington** and **Scoles**.

Afflington farm is a corruption of the Anglo-Saxon "Δelfrun's farm" and is recorded as such in the Domesday Book of 1086. Over the next 150 years this farm became a small hamlet with a substantial manor house and chapel. By the year 1261 it was large enough for King Henry 111 to grant a market and fair. The reason for the expansion and eventual desertion of the village can be directly related to the rise and fall of the marble industry. Deserted by the later middle ages, a brief revival of the stone industry in the seventeenth century was not enough to repopulate the area and by Hutchins' time the site was reduced to the 'foundations of buildings.' The earthworks of the deserted village still cover almost 10 acres of pasture to the east of the present farmhouse. The population of Afflington in the twelfth century has been estimated to be between 150 and 200 inhabitants, in 1803 it was recorded that there were just 83 people living there, mostly quarrymen.

The present house (44) was rebuilt in the middle of the nine-teenth century in imitation of the local seventeenth century style and this building incorporated the west wing of the house built by Giles Green who covenants with the Lady Hatton in a lease dated 24 Nov. 1620 to 'bestowe twentie pounds at the leaste in new building a farm-house near the auncient messuage still standing.' Which implies that the building(s) were in need of restoration. From the third edition of Hutchins (1861) we learn that the building was again in need of renovations and that 'the existing farm-house has been lately repaired, when the porch was rebuilt, and its old semicircular arch, which is no doubt coeval with the rest of the edifice, was converted into an equilateral pointed arch in the style of the fourteenth century.'

Scoles Manor (45), is the most interesting of the houses built along the old marble line and it enjoys one of the best situations on the Purbecks, in a natural bowl with an almost unspoilt panoramic view in the direction of Corfe Castle. Originally built by William de Escoville in the thirteenth century, doubtless on the site of an earlier house, what we now see are parts of an early seventeenth century two-storey house with a two-storey porch which has a round headed doorway with a two-light stone mullioned window under a hood-mould to the upper storey above which is set a carved stone with a rope circle in relief. The house (like Afflington and many others) was heavily restored in the nineteenth century.

But here we have a much more interesting survival in the form of two sections of a late thirteenth century wall, which form respectively, parts of seventeenth and nineteenth century outbuildings. The first outbuilding was conjoined with the main house in the late nineteenth century. The section of early walling here has a late-thirteenth century two light lancet window with the heads united under a single hood-mould. One wall of the other outbuilding contains an altered medieval doorway, the jambs probably contemporary with the window, the pointed head and relieving arch later, but still medieval. The window is on the outside wall of the original building, the door on the inside. The outbuilding with the window is to this day (mainly on the evidence of Hutchins) known as the chapel and although there may have been a chapel here these walls are best interpreted as the remains of the south wall of a single storey medieval hall. The continuing alterations to the buildings here are further evidenced by the bee boles in the east wall of the first outbuilding.

The original fortified manor house of **Holditch Court** at Thorncombe was another building similar in plan to Godlingston, but dating from the late fourteenth or early fifteenth century. This also had a single defensive tower at one end. Other parts of the building, associated earthworks, and a fishpond have become more difficult to trace with the expansion and alterations that have taken place within the farmyard. The present farmhouse consists of a sixteenth century gatehouse that was extended in the seventeenth century, doubtless with materials plundered from the remains of the earlier buildings that had become ruinous. Holditch Court shows the development of this style of fortified manor house into the late fourteenth or early fifteenth century but this building sadly did not find a saviour and it is now an ivy-covered ruin incorporated into farm buildings. All that now remains is the stump of the circular tower which is faced with roughly squared flint and has two string courses but is without windows other than occasional arrow slits in the small round angle tower to light the spiral staircase that was once inside it.

Barnston shows the next stage in the development of the medieval house plan and although the site has pre-Conquest origins (the place name deriving from 'Beorn's Farm') the present buildings date from about 1260. Here the ground floor hall at the eastern end was open to the roof with a two-storey solar cross

Thorncombe: Holditch Court.

wing which itself has a two-storey service block to the west. The controversy over the dating of this west wing (the Royal Commission arguing that it was a sixteenth century addition and that the thirteenth century window had been reset at this date) was finally settled when the plaster was removed in the early 1970s. The wall coursing and roof plate were seen to be continuous and another three blocked lancet windows were found in situ on the south elevation *(46)*. There is, however, no evidence for a kitchen within this plan and the likelihood is that this was external to the house in one of the ranges of buildings that are known to have existed within the former walled courtyard. Sadly, the outbuilding(s) '... *which had an appearance of great*

antiquity', Hutchins writes, *'has recently been cleared away'*. In the fifteenth century, the chimneystack on the south side of the hall was added and in the sixteenth century an upper floor was added to the hall and stone mullioned windows inserted into the south face. The medieval gargoyle reset in the south wall of the barn is evidence that the existing barns were built with materials from the demolished building.

Places of Sanctuary

The county has many churches and monastic buildings that were founded before the conquest. The ecclesiastical beginnings of

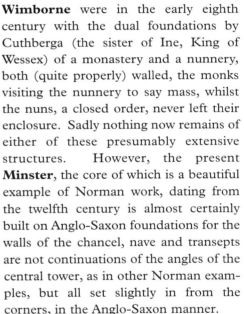

Wimborne were in the early eighth century with the dual foundations by Cuthberga (the sister of Ine, King of Wessex) of a monastery and a nunnery, both (quite properly) walled, the monks visiting the nunnery to say mass, whilst the nuns, a closed order, never left their enclosure. Sadly nothing now remains of either of these presumably extensive structures. However, the present **Minster**, the core of which is a beautiful example of Norman work, dating from the twelfth century is almost certainly built on Anglo-Saxon foundations for the walls of the chancel, nave and transepts are not continuations of the angles of the central tower, as in other Norman examples, but all set slightly in from the corners, in the Anglo-Saxon manner.

This building could well be on the site of the nunnery for King Ethelred, who died near Martin in Hampshire and whose body according to the Anglo-Saxon Chronicle '...*lies at Wimburn Minster ...*' was buried in the Minster church. John Leland tells us, '*The cryptes in the est part of the chirch is an old peace of work. S. Cuthberga was buryid in the north side of the presbyterie. King Etheldrede was byried by her, whos Tumbe was lately repairid, and a marble stone ther layid, with an image of the King in a plate (of) Brasse...*'

The view from Cook Row *(47)* shows the north side of the

church with the junctions of the walls of the nave and transept partially obscured by the addition of the fourteenth century north aisle (which was itself again rebuilt in the restorations that commenced in 1855).

With the exception of the thirteenth century east window, the austere and unbelievably ugly eighteenth century porch, and the eighteenth century alterations to a few windows, most of the present church at **Studland** was built at the end of the eleventh century and on the evidence from excavations carried out during the restorations of 1880–81 possibly on pre-Conquest foundations. These foundations however did not serve the Norman builders well, especially in the case of the tower which was never finished. The walls of the tower are up to six feet thick and the centres of the arches *(48)* beneath the tower bear silent witness in their depression, to some 900 years of pressure from above. The north elevation *(48)* has been least affected by the changes.

A few miles away is the curious late twelfth century building known as **St Aldhelm's Chapel** on St Aldhelm's Head *(48)*. It is square in plan, built of coursed rubble with ashlar dressings, and capped with a pyramidal roof which is covered with stone slates. Hutchins records a Royal Chaplain here in the thirteenth century, but there is really little other evidence to suggest that this building was a chapel. It is incorrectly orientated (the angles set very approximately on the cardinal points) and internally it has a square central clustered pillar with four square rib-vaults and no remains of an altar or piscina. In 1957 part of a Purbeck Marble sarcophagus lid, carved with a raised ornamental cross, dated to between 1250 and 1275 A.D., was found about one mile north-north-east of the building. It was the covering for a stone-lined grave that contained the skeleton of a woman. Nearby were discovered the possible remains of a small building. Perhaps the skeleton was that of a small anchoress and this was her cell? The slab is now in the porch of Worth Matravers Church.

Perhaps confusion has occurred between the anchoress and the site of the chapel; this building may have been simply a seamark and the stunted projection of the central pier through the centre of the roof may once have held a beacon or brazier?

Another fine example of a Norman church is at **Winterborne Thomson** *(49)*. Although many of the earlier Norman churches were built with an apse, this is the sole surviving example in the county. The twelfth century ground plan remains unaltered and most of the walls and the three buttresses of the apse date from that period. The windows have been dated by the Royal Commission to the sixteenth century, but in their present form they probably date from as late as the seventeenth and were even possibly added as late as the early eighteenth century when the church was restored and refitted. At this time it was part of the farm buildings, which may account for the lack of windows on the north side. Here, surely, we have an example of where a slightly earlier style was favoured by the restorer, not in a revivalist spirit, but more from a sense of tradition, born perhaps out of rural isolation. For, in common with so many country areas, little had changed in this small hamlet since the church was built, until the coming of the twentieth century and the motor car.

A fine thirteenth century survival is the dormitory range at **Forde Abbey**, originally a Cistercian monastery founded by 13 monks from that Order's first English foundation (1128) at Waverley in Surrey. The monks had left Surrey to establish a daughter-monastery at Brightley in Devon on the invitation of Sir Richard de Brionis. The land there proved barren and five years later, in 1141, they decided to return to their mother house. On their return journey they were intercepted by Richard's sister, Adelicia, who offered them land at Thorncombe where they stayed and founded Forde. The Dormitory is above the undercroft and 13 lancet windows remain on the west face, those on the east having been removed when the dormitory was cut in two to make servants' quarters. The entrance *(50)* frontage is a mixture of styles from the twelfth to the eighteenth centuries; the earliest surviving masonry from the Norman period is on the inside of the chapter house, which was formerly the chapel of the monastery (the last building on the right of the photograph, surmounted by the clock tower). The outer façades date from the second quarter of the sixteenth century.

LATE MEDIEVAL ARCHITECTURE

The next building that we must take notice of is **Woodsford Castle** (*51*), built between the years 1337 when William de Whitfield was given licence by King Edward III to crenellate (i.e. fortify) his manor house at 'Wyrdesford' and 1391. In the year 1368, Sir John Whitfield, William's son, granted the manor to Sir Guy de Bryan who finished the building between that date and 1391, the year of his death.

Whether or not the buildings extended beyond this single range to form a rectangular castle enclosing a courtyard, is impossible to say now without excavation. Hutchins writes, *'It is probable that an inclosed court probably extended from the western front, including other buildings within its walls, as indicated by the inequalities of the soil in that direction; but the remains are very obscure and irregular, in consequence of the buildings having been erected without sunk foundations.'* Popular tradition, first voiced by Coker, is that the castle was '... *besieged and beaten downe with Ordnance; as a Testimonie wherof they will shewe you, not farre offe in the Warren,* Gunhill, *where they saw the Ordnance planted, and whence it tooke that Name;...'* This would appear to be a

Purse Caundle: Manor House, north front.

piece of folk memory to partly explain why the projected 'castle' was never fully completed, for by the year 1630, the sites of both the castle and settlement of West Woodsford were deserted. Hutchins wrote, *'On the east, a little distance from the castle,...are the marks of dwelling houses and small enclosures, the site of the ancient village, or the residences of the dependants attached to the castle.'* By the eighteenth century the building itself was in a ruinous state and with some internal alteration, converted into a farmhouse and the roof thatched.

The abbey at **Abbotsbury** was founded before the Norman conquest, during the reign of Edward the Confessor, for Benedictine monks. Nothing of this original building remains, its decorative carvings from the late twelfth century and a few architectural features from the thirteenth century having been built into or re-used in many of the extant remains, most of which date from the fourteenth century. The **great barn** (*52*) was built in about 1400, originally 23 bays under a stone slate roof; now, sadly, half of this massive barn is in ruins and the working half thatched. On St Catherine's Hill, to the south-west, stands St Catherine's Chapel (*53*), an unusual building of the late fourteenth century with a broken stone barrel-vaulted roof, a feature which at this late period could only find parallels in the stone-vaulted baronial castles of Scotland. The whole effect of the small building is that of solid mass. Built of local rubble with ashlar dressings, it served as both chapel and seamark; the small stair turret at the north-west corner, rising in its present state above the roofline, could well have been taller and held a beacon or brazier. The three-stage buttresses are massive, united by the string course that runs around the building just above their second stage. They stand as one, proud and defiant, their square embattled pediments further enhancing the Scottish connection as a miniature castle.

The cult of St Catherine of Alexandria was widespread in medieval England, with 61 other churches and chapels dedicated to her, many in similar, slightly isolated hilly situations. Catherine was supposedly a fourth century saint who refused marriage with the Roman emperor saying that she was 'a bride of Christ'. Following an inquisition by 50 philosophers, who tried to convince her of the error of her ways, she retained her Christian beliefs and was martyred. Her body was broken on a wheel (hence Catherine wheel) but when the device broke down, injuring bystanders, Catherine was beheaded; instead of blood, milk flowed from her severed head. St Catherine became the patron saint of all trades that employed the wheel: wheelwrights, spinners and millers, also of nurses and young girls. The latter (and one supposes spinsters generally) would come to the chapel, one day a year, to pray for a husband. Mariners would dip the top sails of their vessels when passing the chapel either praying for a safe voyage out or in grateful thanks for a safe return.

The manor house at **Purse Caundle** was originally a late medieval manor house built by the Long family, one Richard Long having bought land in and around Purse Caundle in 1429. The original building consisted of an open hall and a two-storey solar but these features have been masked by mid-sixteenth century alterations. The original open hall runs roughly north-south, parallel with the modern road and joined the east-west solar wing with its beautiful oriel window, a late-fifteenth century addition, which also over looks this same road. A diagonal buttress incorporated into the east wall probably marks the limit of the original building. In 1528 the estate passed to Richard Hanham whose son William established himself here and amongst other works, made the small additions to the east front of the hall. One of the internal doorway spandrels is carved with his initials. The long south front (*54*) which dates from the early years of the seventeenth century, has a completely unexpected symmetrical E-plan which could easily be taken for an entirely different building. In spite of all these changes, the systematic additions to the structure have merely masked the original building and the various periods of construction can still be fairly easily deciphered.

Sherborne Abbey

Sherborne Abbey is one of the most important monuments in Dorset. Internally it has features that can be

Purse Caundle: Manor House, oriel window.

dated back to the Anglo-Saxon period, but perhaps the finest period in the building's chequered history is the beginning of the fifteenth century. The photograph shows the south elevation of the building which is entirely in the Perpendicular style (*55*); work commenced with the east end (to the right of the photograph) some time between 1420 and 1430. By the year 1437 when the new works had reached the crossing, a fire which followed rioting in the town, halted work and the nave was not completed until the last quarter of the century. The fourteenth century chapels of St Katherine and St Sepulchure (to the left and right of the transept) were rebuilt and incorporated within the general scheme and but for the modern south porch, every-

thing here is in harmony having been conceived as a whole. The huge clerestory, supported with flying buttresses, has windows with six lights and two-centred arches; the main mullions running from top to bottom and the massive eight-light window of the transept, which merely expands the design, are so light and airy that they do not detract from the simpler three-light windows of the south aisle but rather complement them. We should feel honoured that this view is so open and accessible to us and pause when we pass to salute the masons whose skill created it. The nearby **almshouses** of St John the Baptist and St John the Evangelist (*56*), which stand some 60 yards to the south west of the Abbey, were built between 1437 and 1438 and the chapel was completed in 1442. Despite the restorations of 1861, the buildings have remained much the same since that time and are still used for their original purpose, 'the care of 12 poor men and four poor women'. The town should be justly proud of both the abbey church and these almshouses, for the latter is one of the finest examples to have come down to us, another gem.

Athelhampton Hall (*57*) is the finest example of late medieval domestic architecture in the county. It was originally built for Sir William Martyn who was Lord Mayor of London in 1493. This building again also started its life as an open hall with solar end, but here the whole of the original building was flamboyantly supplied with battlements, these being decorative rather than defensive. The four-sided oriel window which now seems to bulge from its junction with the sixteenth century west wing, is also similarly embellished. This west wing had originally formed part of a courtyard with a gatehouse opposite the entrance. This gatehouse and other parts of the building were demolished in 1862 by George Wood who had bought the house in 1848 before he started restoration of the remaining structure. Alfred Cart de Lafontaine, who purchased the house in 1891, continued the restoration and started the re-creation of the gardens (*57*). The circular dovecote can also be dated to the early sixteenth century and although the building no longer serves as a ready supply of food, the fragmenting clouds in the photograph might be mistaken for a flight of birds returning to their nests *(57)*. The farmhouse at **South Idmiston** is reputed to have been built with some of the demolished materials from Athelhampton.

The manor houses at **Sandford Orcas** and **Parnham House,** built in the middle years of the sixteenth century, both convey a very loose style in the lack of symmetry that is displayed in their façades. Sandford Orcas *(58)*, surely one of the most beautiful houses in the county, has come down to us restored but virtually unaltered, the gabled east front with its off-centred gabled porch and two-storey bay window are a sheer delight; another similar but slightly larger bay window is on the south front and these massive windows lit the one-storey hall. However, unlike the previously described 'Hall' houses, Sandford Orcas was designed as a small courtyard house and the solar a mere cellar with a small private room above.

Parnham House like Athelhampton has been much restored and added to. With its rambling entrance front *(59)*, it acts as a good example of the manner in which the architects and masons of the Perpendicular and early Tudor periods viewed the form of the houses that they either constructed or altered to suit their needs; the emphasis being on a collection of individual features rather than a cohesive plan. As we have seen above,

South Idmiston: "Gothic" farmhouse.

the additions at Purse Caundle included a fine oriel window and these alterations were merely added to an existing building without destroying the original established form of the hall house. The slightly larger-than-life hall windows at Sandford Orcas herald a new and bolder style of domestic architecture.

At Parnham Robert Strode entirely rebuilt a house originally built on the site about the year 1400 by John Gerard and which had already been altered and enlarged by William Strode at the end of the fifteenth century. The male line of the Strode family became extinct in 1764 when the house passed into the ownership of the Oglander Family of Nunwell in the Isle of Wight.

For many years after this date the building was untenanted and fell into disrepair. Hutchins' description of the house mentions many buildings that have now gone, including '*the school-house, the gatehouse and the wall about the inner court and the garden*'. Doubtless these were swept away in 1808 when Sir William Oglander took up residence and employed John Nash to make some minor alterations, and two years later to add a dining room and remodel the south front *(60)*. The pinnacles, parapets and gables are mostly the work of Nash and make Parnham what we see today, a rich mixture of Tudor and revivalist architecture in the romantic style.

Wolfeton House, near Charminster, built or at least enlarged in

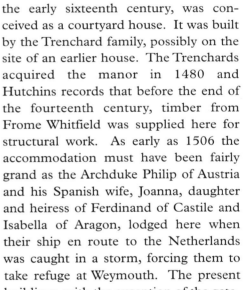

the early sixteenth century, was conceived as a courtyard house. It was built by the Trenchard family, possibly on the site of an earlier house. The Trenchards acquired the manor in 1480 and Hutchins records that before the end of the fourteenth century, timber from Frome Whitfield was supplied here for structural work. As early as 1506 the accommodation must have been fairly grand as the Archduke Philip of Austria and his Spanish wife, Joanna, daughter and heiress of Ferdinand of Castile and Isabella of Aragon, lodged here when their ship en route to the Netherlands was caught in a storm, forcing them to take refuge at Weymouth. The present buildings, with the exception of the gatehouse with its two pseudo-medieval towers of different sizes, and the western corner of the south range which dates from c.1500 *(61)*, are from the mid sixteenth century when the house was greatly extended in a classical style. The large mullioned windows of the present drawing room may be as late as 1600.

Contemporary accounts, drawings and prints, confirm the courtyard arrangement, but sadly many of the buildings have been demolished. Hutchins almost laments their passing: '*On the north side was a small cloister leading to what was the chapel, in which some of the family were married within memory, but it has since been pulled down; and to the west of that a little court.*' This chapel was by the end of the eighteenth century in ruins and demolished in about 1800 and the greater part of the south range and the '*little court*' to the west met the same fate between 1822 and 1828. But we must be thankful that so much is left for us to enjoy (the house is often open to the public) and that we can still easily recognize the '*ivied manor-house, flanked by battlemented towers, and more than usually distinguished by the size of its many mullioned windows*' as Hardy described the house in a *Group of Noble Dames*.

Riding Houses

The county is fortunate to have two riding houses. One of them, the earliest surviving riding house in England, is situated approximately 120 yards north of **Wolfeton**, and was built towards the end of the sixteenth century. The other is at **Wimborne St Giles**, dating from the early years of the seventeenth century. The surviving south-facing block at Charminster has traces of two other blocks or ranges to the north, at right angles. There would also have been another block enclosing a quadrangular courtyard/exercise yard, the other ranges containing barns, additional stabling, tack rooms and possibly a forge and blacksmith's shop. The plan at Wimborne St Giles is more complete but the buildings have later internal alterations and the yard has later walling traversing it. The existing building at **Charminster** of two storeys, the lower storey deep, the upper little more than an attic, is solidly built of ashlar with the exception of the north wall which is composed of squared and coursed rubble. The south front *(62)* is of seven bays divided by buttresses. The bay at the east end, nearly three times the size of the others, contains a blocked central doorcase above which is a lion mask, smaller but similar to those at Lulworth Castle (see below). The adjacent three bays all had square, three-light mullioned windows under labels that fill the distance between the buttresses. Two are now blocked, the third indicated by the remains of the label on either side of a doorway inserted at some later date; probably when the steps were built across the first and second bays at the west end which necessitated the removal of one of the buttresses. The west end has two similar windows under hood-moulds, the east end a single squat window higher up into the gable. **Wimborne St Giles** *(62)* is brick built, the façade symmetrical with nine bays, four of which are gabled with obelisk finials. A moulded ashlar string-course runs along the front, beneath which, on the gabled bays, are four elliptical-headed four-light mullioned windows. Four square-headed single windows stand above the string course and four bullseye windows in the gables. A central elliptical-headed doorway leads to the ground floor. Both of these buildings are in a deplorable state but steps are being taken to restore Charminster, details of which can be had from Nigel Thimbleby at Wolfeton. Of Wimborne St Giles one observer when asked about its current state replied, 'better in this condition than converted to bijou residences'.

ELIZABETHAN ONWARDS

Another example of Perpendicular architecture is the exquisite house known as the **Chantry** at **Trent** on the east side of the churchyard, which was probably built for a chantry-priest in the late fifteenth or early sixteenth century. An impressive and tall building, its south-east elevation facing the road (63) has the original doorway with two-centred arch and square label above. The four principal windows are divided by a central mullion and transom, the upper halves with two centred cinquefoiled heads under square hood-moulds. An almost central projecting chimneybreast bears a tall octagonal chimneystack on this elevation which transforms a functional feature in a manner reminiscent of the circular stack on the Constable's House at Christchurch. There are more magnificent windows on the churchyard elevation and on the faces at either end of the building, as well as features such as small, blank shields enclosed in quatrefoil panels, the gabled ends with projecting chimneybreasts, and smaller octagonal chimney stacks above. So despite minor alterations, the re-set door case on the front façade, and the possibility of restoration to a few of the windows, we are able to feast our eyes on a virtually intact late Perpendicular building.

Bridport: the Museum.

Although there is no documentary evidence for the date of the construction of the Manor House at **Winterborne Clenston,** one of the more peculiar features of the building, the gabled stair turret, would suggest that it was built between 1530–40. This peculiar three-storey octagonal porch/stair turret has a projecting gable supported by corbelled waves of stonework that are splayed out over the angles of the building, this third storey giving access to the attic floors (64). A similar feature is depicted in an eighteenth century engraving on the south front of Wolfeton and a further comparison can be found in the porch on the front of the early sixteenth century building that now houses the **museum** in South Street, Bridport. This latter building was originally known as the **Castle** and tradition has it that it was the house of the chantry-priest of St Leonard.

Edmondsham House is an Elizabethan building, built by Thomas Hussey, who had purchased the manor of Edmondsham in 1563. His initials, a date of 1589, and his carved coat of arms are on the porch. The principal front, with sixteenth century shaped gables in the Dutch manner and all decorated with vases, has retained its overall grandeur but for the nineteenth century remodelling of the principal windows. The lower courses of the porch are of stone but the material for the rest of the building is brick, which on the entrance front is hidden beneath a nineteenth century coat of plaster. Another Thomas Hussey, who died in 1745, added the south-east and north-west wings which are unusual in the fact that the builders retained the semi-circular gable ends at both front and rear. The north-west elevation (65) is well proportioned with a fine early Georgian pediment, and there are similarities with the Georgian façade of **Creech Grange** (66), the latter built to the designs of Francis Cartwright of Blandford between 1738–41. Perhaps he had a hand in the work here at Edmondsham?

Melplash Court was originally a compact house of the early seventeenth century. The photograph shows the north facing entrance front (67). The two gables to the left with the chimney breast between them probably show the full extent of the original building. The larger west wing was added in 1922 to the designs of E. P. Warren and this apparently replaced an earlier wing, but with the present arrangement the seventeenth century dovecot would surely have been too close to the dwelling house?

Hanford House was built (or rebuilt) between 1604 and 1623 for Sir Robert Seymer. A miniature revival of the late medieval courtyard plan, the Royal Commission states that it was built *'on the model of an Italian Palace'*. But here we have an example of an early seventeenth century house, with three-gabled entrance front (67) and pedimented centrepiece, the round-headed arch of which leads through to what was the original courtyard. This was roofed over in 1873, preserving the original elaborate entrance to the hall on the south face, which has the arms of Seymer on a panel surmounted by a cornice with a crouched lion. Handford is now a school and the roofed courtyard has by a simple reversal become the main hall.

The east front has four gables *(68)*, the outer two with slightly offset five-sided, two-storey projections with parapets, the symmetry restored by the round-shafted chimneystacks which add majestic height.

Warmwell House was built for Sir John Trenchard soon after 1618. The Trenchard family of Wolfeton had first acquired the manor in 1526 and the present building incorporates features from an earlier building. The Y-plan of the house is unusual but not unique, the nearest parallel being Newhouse in Whiteparish, Wiltshire which was built contemporaneously. The photograph is of the south front from the south-west *(69)* and shows the two-storey bay window that was added during restoration work in the middle of the nineteenth century, when many of the stone mullions of the other windows were also replaced. But the beauty of the construction lies in the symmetry of the three-gabled front. Here the semicircular gables, surmounted by shaped finials,

Handford House: the covered courtyard.

rise from the roof line on a stepped quadrant. From these steps on either side of the semi-circles, six circular chimneystacks take the eye upwards. As we have seen at Hanford and will see at Anderson Manor, the Dorset architects of the period were very conscious of the effect that the chimneys could add, or otherwise, to the overall balance of their composition.

But an eccentric house needs an eccentric occupant and here lived one John Sadler of whom a clergyman friend had written, '… *it must be owned that he was not always right in his head …* ' Far from being completely deranged, he did have the presence of mind in 1645 to marry Jane, John Trenchard's youngest daughter and co-heiress, who arrived with a fortune of £10,000. Curiously enough, John in the very year of his marriage retired to Warmwell. He had the gift of prophecy and shortly after his occupancy whilst lying ill wrote the unpublished work, '*A Prophecy concerning Plague and Fire in the City of London, certified by Cuthbert Bound, Minister of Warmwell, Dorset'*. He was the author of a few other curious works and died at Warmwell in 1674 in his fifty-ninth year.

By way of contrast, **Court Cottage** at **Pamphill** *(70),* is a simple two-storey building with attics, its walls timber framed and rendered, dating from the early part of the seventeenth century. The photograph of the north-east elevation shows the contemporary five-light window on the gabled north face. The window projects slightly and is supported on shaped brackets. The building was restored recently, its timbers treated over a long period of time and the rendering replaced. A thoroughly good job. The early morning sunshine has caught the east face with low raking light and exposed the underlying timber framework.

Chantmarle *(71)* was built between 1612 and 1623 and the original design was an E-plan manor house but sadly only the central stroke of the letter, the entrance, remains. The building records of the house are still in existence in the form of a manuscript book kept by the owner, Sir John Strode, who had bought the house in 1606. There are extensive quotes from this manuscript in the third edition of Hutchins which also contains an engraving of the original façade. The keystone of the porch has the date 1612 and the single word 'EMMANUEL'. The manuscript explains that the design of the new building, which was a common enough plan during the reign of Queen Elizabeth I, here relates more to the emblem books of the period than to that monarch. Soon after the completion of the building (which is also recorded in Sir John's book) the author moved to Parnham and this house was little used. Both properties in 1764 passed to the Oglander family and Chantmarle became a farmhouse. The building was presumably too big for this purpose and in all probability repairs led to the demolition of the original north and south wings. The building that we see today incorporates at the rear *(71)*, part of the original fifteenth century building as the west wing while the sites of the demolished parts of the E have been replaced by an eighteenth century addition to the northern end of the façade and modern additions to the southern.

Despite being a 'new' house in 1612, the features were those to be found on houses of the early Tudor period; mullion and transom windows, all arched and originally without hood-moulds (as shown on the engraving in Hutchins, mentioned above). From this same engraving we can also observe that a further six gables have been lost and that the semi-circular form of the oriel window was echoed in two two-storey bay windows on the east faces of the wings.

Similar arched fenestration but without the transoms can be seen at **Puncknowle Manor** *(72)*. Here we can see the continuing use of an earlier style down to the middle of the seventeenth century. Although the main body of the building dates from the nineteenth century, the symmetrical entrance front of the old T-shaped house is a wonderful survival. The hipped, roofed porch sitting squarely in the centre, its roofline falling just short of

Buckland Newton: Manor House.

that of the main block, contains a double staircase clockwise and anti-clockwise, the two sections joining to give access to the upper floor. This staircase accounts for the grand proportions, the two round-headed, single-light windows illuminate the two flights and the three-light window the landing. The round head of the porch doorcase leads to a barrel vault beneath the staircases. The symmetry is completed by the four three-light windows of the main block; all of the windows have hood-moulds.

The photograph is taken from just outside the eighteenth century gateposts with the tower of the church just visible to the right.

Little other than a few cosmetic changes can have been made to alter this view since they were built.

We will diversify a little here to examine the small manor house at **Buckland Newton**. One of the rainwater heads is dated 1803 and the house has been seen as an early example of the Tudor revival movement. However, further examination of the extant features may lead us to a different conclusion. Tall symmetrical front, mullioned and transomed windows with hood-moulds, gables at both ends, topped with finials; surely here we have the remodelling of an already existing Tudor house, perhaps after a fire or a long period of disuse.

Retrospective rebuilding and design is not unknown in the county. The east front of **Creech Grange** *(73)* is a convincing pastiche of an early Elizabethan E-plan house which was built (or rebuilt) between 1846 and 1847. A piece of pure Tudor revival architecture can be seen at **Compton House** *(74)*, Over Compton (for many years the home of Worldwide Butterflies). It was built of Ham Hill rubble and ashlar, by John Pinch (the younger) of Bath, sometime around 1839. It is a true pastiche of the E-plan; a single-storey porch at the centre, two-storey embattled bay windows with pinnacled, stepped gables on the wings which are a continuation of the embattled parapet between them, and tall chimney stacks to complete the picture. All this is set in parkland with space to set off its grandeur.

Iwerne Minster was turned by James Ismay, the Lord of the Manor, into a model village in the 1920s. Many of the existing houses received imitation Tudor half-timbering. **The Homestead** (now called **The Oak House**) *(75)* was gifted by Ismay to the village as a clubhouse in 1921. The building was designed by Baillie, Scott & Beresford and utilised much reclaimed genuine Tudor material. The porch, which seems to have been lifted in its entirety and reset here, dates from c.1500.

Lulworth Castle and the Welds

The death knell of the medieval castle was the cannon. Castle building reached its zenith in the early fifteenth century, but just when you think it's all over, along comes Thomas Howard, Third Viscount Bindon of Bindon Abbey, who builds another one! **Lulworth Castle** (76) was built in 1608 as a lodge for occasional use, the fashion for building mock castles being quite the thing in the reign of James I. Other examples are the late fifteenth century Wickham Court in Kent; Mount Edgecumbe, Cornwall, built in 1546; Sherborne New Castle, here in Dorset, built some time after 1592; and Longford Castle in Wiltshire, built in 1578–9. All have a distinct military character but without the real solidity that their design implies. Lulworth Castle is built of brick and faced with Purbeck and Portland rubble with ashlar. In 1641 it was bought by Humphrey Weld and has remained in that family until this day. Designed as an austere building it had little decoration save for the two human masks and lions' heads that are either below or flanking the windows. Here, as at Chantmarle and other retrospectively built houses in Dorset, the windows have arched lights. When Humphrey Weld bought the castle it was unfinished. His descendants added the triumphal arch over the entrance on the east elevation some time around 1700 and by 1765 had extended the terrace on the east front around the north and south sides, the whole of which was reconstructed in 1776. In 1929 a fire gutted the castle and for many years it was overgrown and in a ruinous condition. Present members of the Weld family have taken the necessary steps to both conserve and preserve this wonderful piece of seventeenth century whimsy for future generations to enjoy whilst building for themselves a smaller pastiche of a pastiche nearby.

Within the grounds of the castle is the **Roman Catholic Chapel of St Mary** (77) built for Thomas Weld in 1786–7 to the designs of John Tasker. Tradition has it that King George III told Weld he could carry out his plans for a Catholic chapel on the understanding that the finished building did not *look* like a chapel. Tasker was more than man enough for the task and a building that looked less like a chapel would be difficult to imagine. From a distance it has the appearance of a grand summerhouse (and who could not expect such a thing given the Quixotic nature of the castle) but as you move closer, the building looks more like a dwelling house. The shape is a domed quatrefoil with four rectangular stone piers, with niches, surmounted by artificial stone urns where the cusps of the quatrefoil meet, which flatten the full circular forms into bows. A rectangular abutment for a vestry and staircase lies *behind* the high altar, which faces north. Entrances occur on the north and south faces, both with Tuscan porches and urns, the south being more elaborate; here the porch is set in an arched wall-recess and flanked by niches containing urns.

As if these two delightful buildings were not enough, north-north-west of the castle are the North Lodges (78), another of Lulworth's charms. The pair of triangular ashlar-faced embattled buildings, dated 1785, stands between the two gate piers bearing the Weld Arms, to the right and left are carstone rubble walls with embattled parapets and more (smaller) round towers. With their circular angle towers and round-headed windows, the lodges mimic the castle. These lodges and the chapel ably demonstrate the family's continuing interest in the original theme of the mock castle, almost 150 years after the original purchase. But times change, this is no longer the main entrance to the castle and the pair stand (albeit restored) somewhat neglected and slightly forlorn beside a public footpath. Looking through them you can glimpse the castle, approximately one mile away.

The Weld family throughout their occupancy seem to have been imbued with a concern for the future of the estate and its buildings. In 1808 when the formal gardens around the house were removed, the lodge gate (78) that formerly stood at the entrance (and which is the same date as the original castle) was not destroyed but moved to a new position beside the Wareham road. The engraved view of Lulworth in Hutchins' shows this lodge gate (and the gardens) in their original positions.

The new house at **Bindon Abbey** (78) built by Thomas Weld senior between 1794 and 1798, was primarily built, it seems, as a Roman Catholic chapel, the orientation being east-west, but it was not registered as a place of worship until 1852. Between 1886 and 1893 the lower floor served as a small Roman Catholic school while the upper room was used as a chapel. It has now been completely converted to a dwelling house. The photograph shows the north-west elevation of the house which is built of Purbeck rubble with ashlar quoins. The spacious upper floor is lit by three three-light windows, the tracery with crosses, while the lower storey has meaner windows with hood-moulds and a slightly incongruous embattled central porch. The gable ends of the roof are pinnacled. The overall impression is probably what Weld intended, a pastiche of pieces that might have been retrieved from the ruins of the original Bindon Abbey, which at the time when this house was new were much more in evidence.

Another branch of the Weld family lived at **Chideock**. Between 1870–72 Charles Weld began building the **Roman Catholic chapel** of Our Lady of Martyrs and St Ignatius to his own design. It was finished in 1884 with the addition of a chancel and transepts designed by J. S. Hansom, the whole building enclosed in a pre-existing barn where clandestine services had previously been conducted. Most of the carving, decoration and the capitals are Weld's work. The entrance front is in the Byzantine style, the interior *(79)* is light, airy and colourful and has the feel of a small Italian church. The chapel has a pair of censers that were designed by Pugin. In 1880 Weld also designed and built the family mausoleum in Chideock churchyard, a Greek Byzantine cross with a central tower which has a pyramid roof; he also carved the crucifix on the west end.

Anderson Manor *(80)* was built for John Tregonwell, the rainwater heads here bearing his initials and the date 1622. Deep plum coloured Dorset brick alternates with vitrified brick burnt to a rich purple colour on every third course, with limestone dressings; the windows are of stone cross mullion and transom design, with the exception of those in the gables that have hood-moulds but are without a transom. The gables have ball finials and two groups of lozenge-shaped chimneystacks set equidistantly between the gables. Another porch in the form of an octagon, five sides proud of the building, the other three imagined in the lower end of the hall, an octagonal variation on the entrance porch of Waterston and a rationalization of the earlier porch at Winterborne Clenston. The house is surrounded with greenery which adds an almost esoteric

Winterborne Anderson: St Michael.

quality to its undoubted beauty. All of these features and the perfect classic proportions make Anderson Manor one of the most beautiful of the smaller Tudor manor houses in Britain. Its fortunes have not always been as good, however. For a long period during the nineteenth century when not used as a residence, it was neglected and fell into disrepair, to be saved from total ruin by Mrs Gordon Gratrix. After purchasing it in 1910 she set about the restoration of the house and its surroundings, supplying the present drive and restoring the original garden plans.

The small nearby church dedicated to St Michael was built in 1889 on the foundations and to the same plan as the building then existing which doubtless had fallen into disrepair. Now, just over a century later, this building has the look of one that recent time has passed by as it proudly rises above the plethora of vegetation that surrounds it. But caution should be our watchword for the early signs of decay are here; some guttering loose, paint flaking on the wooden surfaces, and even the unusual churchyard gate has a loose top rail. I fear that some of this original woodwork will not be with us much longer, which would be a sad finale.

Woolbridge Manor appears in Hardy's *Tess of the d'Urbervilles* as Wellbridge farm and it was here that Angel Clare took his bride for their honeymoon. Hardy altered the family and place names only slightly in his novels and the owners were the Turberville family when the present house was built, having acquired the property towards the end of the sixteenth century. The original house was much older and prior to the Dissolution of the Monasteries had belonged to Bindon Abbey. This, with its brick north façade *(81)* like Anderson, is an early example of the use of that material in the county. The rest of the building, with the exception of the upper parts of the gables of the south face, is mostly built of stone. The fenestration of the north front is interesting and individual. The narrow niches to either side of the three-light transomed windows on the second storey match those on either side of the porch entrance, and the six brick relieving arches over the rendered brick string course show that there were two smaller windows to either side of the two larger windows which remain. The round windows either side of the porch, along with the roundel on the porch, which contains a re-set piece of stone with the date 1635 and the initials I.S., are later additions of about 1670. More niches on the chimneystacks helps to give some idea of the appearance of the original front.

The house is usually photographed from the other side of the River Frome and this entrance front is perhaps not so well known as it should be. At the time of writing, the house is open for bed and breakfast so perhaps more people will see this exquisite piece of Dorset's architectural history.

Waterston House was built originally in the second quarter of the seventeenth century but was severely damaged by fire in 1863 and subsequently rebuilt. It is now impossible to determine the original plan of the house and the only remaining features of the original building are the south front and part of the east front. The south front *(82)* is the most interesting with the semi-circular turret-like bay raised above a square Doric doorcase which has a round-headed archway and moulded architrave. This elevation is built of diapered brickwork, rendered above the first storey, the bay with a chequer-work of brick and ashlar blocks, all dressed with Ham Hill stone. The four main windows, on the first and second storeys of the outer gables, are two-light with transom, those within the gables have hood-moulds but are without transom. The fenestration is similar in design to the front of Anderson Manor, save for the pediments above the second-floor windows. The top section of the semi-circular bow is topped with a parapet and the gable behind has a single light with a round head. The three gables are linked by arched openings in the false parapet.

The east front *(83)* has two projecting gables, one near the centre, the other at the south end, both almost certainly parts of the original house. The gable near to the centre has a re-set classical frontispiece dated 1586.

The date and plan of the original manor house at **West Stafford** are unknown. Originally known as Frome House, it served as the manor house for Frome Billet, a lost Dorset village that was deserted and depopulated before the year 1500. The Long family held manors in this area and in 1613 sold both this manor and the manor of Stafford, with its farm, to John Gould a Dorchester merchant. Gould, who also owned property in Dorchester and Fordington, died in 1630. His son, another John, is generally credited as the builder of the new manor house, the present east-facing block *(84)*, the porch of which is dated 1633. This E-plan house is symmetrical but for the fenestration of the south wing where the new house incorporates part of the earlier sixteenth century manor house. Once again we see arched, mullioned windows similar to Chantmarle and Puncknowle, here with hood-moulds but without transoms. The façade seems somehow to be stretched, leaving space for two bays either side of the gabled porch. The two bays next to the porch have gabled attics which rise to the height of the wing gables and slightly dwarf the porch gable, but this somehow adds a flowing rhythmic quality and now that this has ceased to be the business front, this side of the building almost seems to relax into the garden. We will learn more of the west front which was built to the designs of Humphrey Repton by Benjamin Ferrey between the years 1848 and 1850 subsequently.

Parts of **Hammoon Manor House** date back to the first half of the sixteenth century but the main ashlar-faced south façade *(84)* dates from the latter half of that same century. The slightly larger-than-life porch, is more classical with a half round-headed entrance arch raised on banded columns of the Tuscan order and a semi-circular ornamental gable. It is a later addition of about 1600, but fashioned with a three-light, arched, mullioned window beneath a hood-mould which emulates the style of the other windows on this façade. One of the greatest attractions of the house is the thatched roof, unusual for so large a house, but not unique as we have seen at Woodsford Castle, although at Hammoon it may well have been the chosen material from the early seventeenth century.

Mapperton is recorded in the Domesday Book and a manor house in some form has probably been in existence on this site since Norman times. The church was originally built in the twelfth century, but of this era only parts of the chancel and the tower arch remain. Like the manor house itself, the structure and appearance of the building have both been restored and modified over the centuries. Indeed it would appear that it was purposely altered, by removal of the west tower, to better fit the design of the manor house and its associated buildings. Here is set out before us one of the best examples of a manorial group in the county; the main block, which faces east *(85)*, is the underbelly of an extended U where the now towerless church forms the south wing, the form of the letter further extended by the north and south stables on the opposite side of the road.

The house was built by Robert Morgan (Hutchins in the eighteenth century saw an inscription to that effect in the hall) but all that remains of his house is the north wing and the underlying plan of the east range. The windows of the north range date from about 1550–1560; the window in the gable on the west face has four-arched lights with hood-mould. The angles of this façade have semi-octagonal buttresses surmounted with twisted pinnacles on which stand heraldic beasts. In the seventeenth century Richard Broadrepp, who had married into the Morgan family, remodelled the west façade with a central porch and two-storey bay-windows at either end, once again the classic E-plan. The stables were added in 1670 when other modifications were made, including the remodelling of the north face of the west wing, once again classical symmetry in five bays. The central bay projects forward and is topped with a curious length of almost free-standing balustrade, perhaps merely a pastiche of the balustrading over the west front, with a simple pedimented doorcase below.

High Hall, at Pamphill, dating from about 1670, is built of brick with ashlar dressings, though the brick has been for many years rendered over. The roof is tiled with stone slates on the verge. The south front *(86)* (the original entrance front) is symmetrical and of five bays with a flight of steps up to a central pedimented doorway. Stone plat-bands just above the window sills of the two main storeys divide the vertical front into three. The windows of the lower main storey are round-headed with blind lunettes and five equally spaced dormer windows in the roof bring the composition to its logical conclusion. The bow-fronted addition to the left of the building added in 1885, was designed by Crickmay & Son, of Dorchester.

Chettle House *(87)* was built by Thomas Archer for George Chafin in 1710, according to Hutchins, but the consensus of opinion is that on stylistic grounds it was probably built some ten or fifteen years later. Despite this minor controversy it is without

doubt one of the finest examples of English Baroque architecture in the British Isles. The attribution to Archer comes partly from family history and from the treatment of the original entrance front on the east elevation.

The house has undergone many changes but thankfully it is now, with the exception of a cupola (which is said to have been removed in the nineteenth century) and the balustrading on the curved walls of the rounded bays, remarkably close to the original design. For a period of some thirty years after the death of the Revd William Chafin (George's son) in 1818 the building was vacant and fell into a ruinous state. In the mid 1840s Edward Castleman moved here from Wimborne (his father had purchased the house in 1826) and set about restoring it. The 'restorations' included the lowering of the curved ends of the house to a single storey above the basements as depicted in Pouncy's *Dorsetshire Photolithographically Illustrated* of 1856. The curved second storeys were replaced in 1912 and the balustrading added to them. The photograph shows the east front of nine bays, those at either end curved, the three in the middle projecting and rising above the second storey. The bays are defined by brick pilasters capped with Chilmark stone. On the central projection the rounded heads of the windows have elaborate keystones and the brick pilasters between them are banded with stone. The full balance of the front is supplied by the two flights of stone steps which serve both ground level and basement.

Chettle village remains remarkably rural with a simple village shop and the newly refurbished eighteenth century Lodge turned into a fine hotel and restaurant called the Castleman, perhaps in gratitude for that family's work to preserve Chettle House? On the approach to the house there is a superb example of an early nineteenth century **granary** on staddle stones which stands in very stately fashion behind a recently restored pond *(88)*.

For many years the building of Chettle House was attributed to Sir John Vanbrugh who designed Eastbury House in the early years of the eighteenth century and tradition has it that he was also responsible for the design of **Horton Church** tower *(89)* which was built in 1722. The ashlar tower is of two stages defined by an ashlar band, the first with a beautifully proportioned round-headed window, the second with a bullseye window which when visible must have been a delight to behold, but alas, someone has seen fit to fill this feature with an oversize clock! The second stage rises to a modillion cornice and a parapet which supports a pyramidal spire with triangular dormers (*lucarne jacobine*). The photograph shows the north faces of the tower and the north transept, the rebuilding of the latter being completed in 1755 using mainly reclaimed fifteenth century material. Above the fifteenth century doorcase is an eighteenth century round-headed window and in the gable above that a bullseye window, similar to those in the tower, but lack of space here (or perhaps someone merely mimicking a great architect) means that this façade lacks the majesty that the tower had before the insertion of the clock.

Follies and Curiosities

A short distance away stands **Horton Tower**, *(90)* a folly of about 1750. The brick tower is triangular with circular turrets capped by ogee domes on the angles, with pediments between them for the first four storeys and the upper two storeys hexagonal. Humphrey Sturt of Horton is deemed to have built the tower which is called 'Horton Observatory' on Isaac Taylor's map of Dorset (1765) and although the building may have been designed for that purpose, popular tradition favours the notion that Sturt (who removed to Crichel) built it to view the hunt when he grew too old to participate.

Another eighteenth-century curiosity can be seen nearby at **Woodlands**, the **Round House** *(91)*. The eighteenth century part consists of a rectangular building with two apsidal ends, orientated north-south; an east wing was added in the early nineteenth century and another to the west about 1850. There is evidence that prior to this there were single-storey wings. The apses originally had three uniform windows and the side walls had windows at the same height. The height difference in floor levels (compared to buildings of a similar date) means that the upper floor is more akin to an attic. One possibility is that people were employed on the upper floor at some industry that needed good light to achieve this the ability to move with the sun would be an advantage. Think of the 'top shops' in Islington and other parts of London where tailors worked in small well-lit studios and you have a reference point. Perhaps the occupants were Flemish or Dutch Huguenots driven here by religious persecution?

Georgian Glories

Dorset possesses two Georgian townscapes and for two entirely different reasons. The '*Dreadfull fire*' that consumed most of the town of **Blandford Forum** on 4 June, 1731, '*broke out in a tallow-chandler's shop in the northern outskirts of the town at about two in the afternoon at which time the wind blew strong at N. West which carried the Flame over towards the East end of the Church, and set fire to all the buildings in that Tract, so that not less than 20 houses were on fire within a ¼ of an hour.*' The wind direction changed towards… '*ye adjacent villages of Brianstone and Blandford St Mary, so that all before the Wind in the space of an hour was on Fire, and the Thatch'd buildings soon consumed.*' The church survived the first day of the fire '*til abt 2 in the morning, then broke out in the middle Isle under the lead, where 'twas impossible to extinguish it without Engines which were already burnt many hours before,…*' By the morning the town must have consisted of a mass of smouldering, hot ruins, '*ye church was entirely destroy'd ye poor remains being scarcely fit for a Foundation.*'

This narrative is printed on an engraved plan of the town '*with the adjacent villages … describing the damages in each place…*' which was measured, drawn and engraved by John and William Bastard, the surviving members of the firm of Bastard & Company, shortly after the fire. Their father, Thomas Bastard, had established himself as a joiner some years previously and held the office of Bailiff in 1713. Equipped as the brothers were as architects, surveyors, builders and joiners, the firm was appointed to survey and rebuild the town; this they achieved over the following thirty years and the result is a compact eighteenth century market town. They were responsible for most but not all of the major buildings. One of the few buildings to survive the fire is the **Old House** *(91)* in The Close behind East Street, a red brick house of about 1600 with a roof that is for the greater part covered with stone slates and topped with tiles. The front elevation always appears slightly odd and lop-sided, as if the kitchen wing at the side had been added at a later date, upsetting the symmetry of the building. The construction is all of the same date, however, so perhaps this wing was added as an afterthought, for the building shares the same step-hipped roof.

Much of the new Georgian building, especially the houses, was with brick, mostly red with the occasional blue. For the more important civic buildings the brothers used stone. The **Town**

Hall *(92)*, which has the inscription *'BASTARD, ARCHITECT, 1734'* carved above the central window, is of Portland Ashlar and the church, which was completed in 1739, has walls of Greensand ashlar with dressings of Portland and Ham Hill stone. The compact fire monument at the east end of the **Market Place**, designed by John Bastard and with the date 1760 on the tympanum of the pediment, carries an inscription concerning the fire and the rebuilding of the town, risen *'like the PHAENIX from it's Ashes, to its present beautiful and flourishing state.'* The inscription also records that the new water supply for the town is housed here *'to prevent by a timely Supply of Water, (With God's Blessing) the fatal Consequences of FIRE hereafter …'*

The only major building of the post-fire buildings to be rendered in stucco is **The Old Greyhound Inn** in the market place *(93)*, which was completed in about 1735. The Bastard brothers owned the Inn at that time and were presumably responsible for its design and construction. It has fine Corinthian details on five pilasters that rise to the central triangular pediment.

The other Georgian town is **Weymouth**. The rise of the town as a resort where the new pastime of sea bathing could be enjoyed was some twenty years prior to the first visit of King George III in 1789. Having taken a great liking to the town, the king spent

Blandford Forum: the fire monument.

his long summer holidays here for the next sixteen years. This royal patronage brought the town wealth, social standing and the need for new building development. New terraces abounded and the half mile of terraced esplanade soon took on the aspect for which this 'new' town is now so famous.

The terraces sometimes turn corners and the stuccoed front of the house directly behind the statue of King George at the entrance to St Mary Street *(94)*, built about 1805, is a wonderful example of the solution to that problem, the slightly bulbous look coming from the shallow bowed windows of the three storey façade.

Encombe House near Corfe Castle is another long, low building in the manner of Vanbrugh, solidly built of Purbeck ashlar some time after 1734 for John Pitt. Pitt was an amateur architect and may well have designed Encombe himself. The photograph *(95)* shows a fête in progress before the old north entrance front; the figures help to give scale to the architectural composition in which every feature has been designed to accentuate the low nature of the building.

Two more fine mid-eighteenth century houses in the county are **Came House** at **Winterborne Came**, built by Francis Cartwright, of Blandford Forum, in 1754; and **Ranston** at **Iwerne Courtney** which was built one year before.

All that remains of the house built for Thomas Ryves at Ranston in is the classically proportioned west front *(96)*. The Ryves family of Blandford had owned the estate from 1545 and this building was erected on the site of an earlier seventeenth century house, traces of which can be seen in the basement. The front is of five bays. Four Portland stone Corinthian pilasters crowned with a pediment emphasize the three central bays and a double flight of stone steps complete the symmetry. The steps that were replaced during the 1960s, coupled with the demolition of some nineteenth century additions, have returned this aspect of the house to its former beauty and the shallow light of evening captured in the photograph, illuminating the façade, serves to outline the grandeur of the design and construction.

Came House was the high point of Cartwright's career and his most ambitious project, completed a few years before his death in 1758. Fittingly, beneath his marble monument in Blandford St Mary church are two scrolls of paper, one which depicts the front of the house. The view is of the south front *(97)*, the original entrance front with five bays. The central bay projecting slightly forward is topped with a pediment above a modillion cornice, which continues around the top of the house and supports a balustrade. The central French windows on the ground floor are beneath a pediment with entablature, supported by Ionic columns. The entablature repeats over the windows to either side where it is carried on pilasters; above this is a central round-headed window flanked by two squat square-headed windows with a broken entablature, again supported on pilasters with Corinthian style capitals, which allows the centre of the circular window to rise to a respectable height above them. Another squat window in the pediment above stretches the design and brings it to a triumphal close. In the shadow to the right of the façade is the contemporary kitchen wing and to the left an impressive conservatory that was added in the middle years of the nineteenth century.

Smedmore House, like so many country houses, has two fronts. The original house on this site was built by Sir William Clavell in the early seventeenth century. Early in the next century the whole building was remodelled with a south-west elevation, most of which is still extant. It is a simple symmetrical façade of five bays rising two storeys to a parapet. Alas the building of the new north front destroyed the symmetry by taking away the left hand bay (the two windows of which appear to have been reset on the back wall of the new front). The wing was added to the right hand end c.1800. The north front *(98)* was built in 1761 and the block contains a new entrance hall and reception rooms.

Smedmore House: the south-west elevation.

Clavel Tower, which overlooks Kimmeridge Bay *(99)* was built about 1820 by the Revd John Richards who assumed the name Clavell when he inherited Smedmore in 1817. The solitary folly is now a ruined tower of three stages with a semi-basement, a colonnade of Tuscan columns circling the lower storey above it. It is rather picturesquely crumbling away and the last twenty five years have witnessed the loss of the mock machicolations that rose from the parapet.

The finest eighteenth century church in Dorset is **St George**

Reforne, in the Isle of Portland, designed and built by Thomas Gilbert between 1754 and 1766, its situation, almost on top of the island, west of Easton, adding to its grandeur and eccentricity. In this position and without the tower, the nave, pedimented transepts and the flattened dome over the crossing, have the appearance of an observatory *(100)*.

The former **Congregational Chapel** in Skinner Street, **Poole**, now the United Reform Church, (who could mistake this from the frieze over the porch) *(100)* was built in 1777, a north vestry added in 1814, extended to the east in 1823 and the pedimented porch supported on six Doric columns was added in 1833. The main construction is of brick, the side walls hung with slates. The west front, remarkably in this twenty-first century, is still easily visible and is composed of five bays. The windows, with pointed heads and Y tracery on the first two stages, are of a similar shape but blind on the third stage, their heads in an elongated stepped and shaped gable with obelisks on the steps. The date 1777 is in a cartouche above the central window of the second stage. Another remarkable survival considering the intensive development of this area of Poole.

The thatched lodge at **Stanbridge** *(101)* and **Umbrella Cottage** in **Lyme** *(102)* are both examples of the cottage orné. These were initially built as lodges at the entrance to large estates when the manufacture of the picturesque was fashionable. The first, built in 1809 as one of the lodges to Gaunt's House, is a good example of this rustic style and is similar to the second at Lyme. But where is the house served by Umbrella Cottage; perhaps this is just a seaside folly? At **Chantmarle** the present entrance drive skirts around the twin thatched lodges *(103)* which were made redundant for that purpose some years ago. Also in Lyme on Marine Parade, **Madiera Cottage** and **Little Madiera**, a fine pair of early eighteenth century cottages, with semi-circular bow-windows.

Every Dorset village, in common with most English villages, has an 'Old Rectory'. In common with most old rectories the **Old Rectory** at Edmondsham, near Cranborne *(104)* is strictly speaking the 'New Rectory'. When the main road through the village, which conveniently (or perhaps inconveniently) passed the door of Edmondsham House, was altered and the grounds of that house extended in 1900, the real Old Rectory that stood within the present grounds was demolished and the Rectory moved to this new site, where an existing eighteenth century house was extended to what we see today. The eighteenth century west range, of rendered brick and partly tile-hung, had been the subject of improvements in the first half of the nineteenth century, with the addition of the bay window and the blocking of some windows and a door on the west front, all of which have, thankfully, now been replaced. The old saying is that curiosity killed the cat, but Edward (the cat here) seems oblivious to this notion.

Kingston Lacy House *(105)* was built originally for Sir Ralphe Bankes between 1663 and 1665. The house was originally constructed of brick with stone dressings and had mullioned and transomed windows which survive only on the west front. In 1835, when William Bankes asked Charles Barry to alter the house, he encased it in Caen stone with Portland stone dressings.

The **Old Manor**, formerly Ilsington House, near to the church in **Puddletown** *(106)* has the distinction of being the only William and Mary house in the county. The nucleus of the present house, the central portion with hipped roofs and panelled chimneystacks, was built for Samuel Rolfe in the late seventeenth century. In the nineteenth century the brick walls were rendered with stucco and the North porch added. Comprehensive restoration and refurbishment at the end of the twentieth century allowed closer inspection of the construction which has led the present owner to the conclusion that the present building is on the site of an earlier sixteenth century house and this prompted his decision to change the name.

Stable Manor at **Chalmington** near Chantmarle *(107)* is a difficult building to categorise, as it is effectively the stable block of the adjacent manor house, a building with vague Tudor revival pretensions. The stables were converted to a dwelling house soon after the turn of the twentieth century. When the photograph was taken, the rendered front was painted in a faded green, it had

been stripped of the ivy and other climbing plants (ready for a make-over) and still bore the scars. It had taken on a peculiar form of beauty, so perhaps we arrived just in time.

Dorset contains many Gothic revival buildings, both ecclesiastical and secular. Apart from those described elsewhere, I will treat the following examples (as far as is possible) in chronological order. The view of **St Nicholas Church** *(107)* Moreton, built by James Frampton in 1776, shows the apsidal sanctuary with five three-light windows with intersecting cusped tracery, all joined together by a continuous two-centred hood-mould, the short horizontal links having shields below them carved with the arms of Frampton. The faces of the pew (a small section of the building so named because it contains the Frampton pew) and the north aisle, this latter rebuilt in 1840–41 reusing some of the old material, all have similar windows with shield stops, as does the east face of the tower. The cusped motif appears again as a roundel on the panelled parapet that runs all around the church.

Joseph Damer's Mansion next to the church at **Milton Abbey** *(108)* was built to the designs of Sir William Chambers in 1774. It is in the Gothic manner in imitation of the church.

The inspiration for the north-west façade of **Pulham Rectory** *(109),* built c.1800, may well have come from Milton Abbey. Its three-bay front is symmetrical. The central bay is slightly recessed with a three-sided porch, the entrance doorway has a pointed head and label, and both sides of the porch have narrow lancet windows. The fenestration reduces slightly from three-light, four-centred windows with lancets either side of them under a common label, to a similar window without lancets under a hood-mould, then to elliptical lights for the attic rooms. At the top, there is an embattled parapet, the crenellations of the outer bays much larger than the smaller central bay. The theme and general feeling continue with the wing that projects to the south. On a hot summer day the building has a fairytale quality and far from seeming small, appears larger than life.

Highcliffe Castle, near Christchurch, was built between 1830 and 1834 to the designs of John William Donthorne. It replaced an Adam house of 1773 and here is a happy mixture of two eras of Gothic, the new and the French original. The house seems to have no real plan but simply ambles in all directions *(110),* the architect fitting his new work around the reclaimed French material that the owner Charles Stuart (Lord Stuart de Rothesay) had bought from various mediaeval sites in Normandy. One of the most imposing and beautiful pieces being the magnificent oriel window over the entrance porch *(111)*. This originally graced the entrance front of La Grande Maison at Les Andeleys, one of the few domestic buildings etched by John Sell Cotman for his *Architectural Antiquities of Normandy* published in 1822. Another French lithograph, published in 1825 depicts the 'destruction' of this same building.

The little church at **Winterborne Clenston** *(112)* was built by Lewis Vulliamy in 1840 in what one might today term a politically incorrect Gothic style. Cruciform in plan, the west tower with a debased form of broach spire, the walls are composed of flint and ashlar in bands, with stone dressings, the roof with stone slates. The overall effect of the stone and flint is pleasing but the doors and windows are slightly too large for the general scale of the building and although the panelled surround with its fleur-de-lys finial and artificial stone trophy-of-arms should look looming and out of place, somehow it does not *(112)*.

R. C. Carpenter rebuilt the church at Monkton Wyld in 1848–49 in good fourteenth century Gothic and gave it a stone broach spire, a feature that would be more at home in Northamptonshire. He also built the Rectory (now **Monkton Wyld Court**) a

slightly sombre building. The entrance front *(113)* has a circular window high in the gable, the tracery bearing another smaller circle containing a quatrefoil and the windows of the garden front *(113)* all good facsimiles of fourteenth century windows, those of the lower storey repeating the quatrefoils in their tracery. There is little attempt at symmetry here, one gable end with a two-storey bow, the other with a one-storey porch. The unfortunate dormer windows and roof light are obvious 'improvements'. The building will stand comparison with the work of Benjamin Ferrey and Pugin.

The church at **Kingston** *(114)*, near Corfe Castle, was designed and built by George Edmund Street between 1873 and 1880 at an estimated cost of £70,000. With no expense spared, it is not difficult to see why this is the high point of his career. It is a piece of thirteenth century Italianate Gothic, cruciform, apsidal, with a tall central tower and transepts, the north with a round stair turret, the design of which is copied from Christchurch. All the windows with the exception of the rose window on the west end and the small window of the south transept are medieval lancets. The west end has a narthex, or covered porch, running along its length; the decoration of the portal and other carvings were executed by Milburn, under the direction of Street (and in the case of the capitals) from models in clay made by him. The interior contains a staggering amount of Purbeck marble.

BENJAMIN FERREY (1810-1880)

A Short Life of the Architect and Brief Descriptions Of His Work In Dorset

Benjamin Ferrey was one of the leaders of Tudor and Gothic revival architecture in England. Apprenticed to the elder Pugin, and an almost exact contemporary of his son Augustus Welby Northmore Pugin (1812–52), he was greatly influenced by both in his long career. His indebtedness to them can be felt in his *Recollections of Pugin*, published in 1861. His work has a much lighter and more easily approachable aspect than that of the younger Pugin whose work tends to have an austere quality about it.

Pugin was a sombre, tragic genius, described by Trappes Lomax as a '*Medieval Victorian*'. He devoted his life to the study and recreation of Gothic art and architecture, and having converted to the Roman Catholic faith in 1835, developed an abhorrence of any non-Catholic art. He lived in his latter years at Ramsgate in Kent where he built his own house and church. Ferrey adequately describes his later life as being '*of almost monastic regularity…*' with his daily studies and devotions in both library and church filling his waking hours from six in the morning until midnight.

Ferrey, by way of contrast, was an Anglican who found relaxation and release in music, particularly church music (he had a pleasing baritone voice) and in his other pastime, painting in watercolours. His private life is summed up in his entry in the *Dictionary of National Biography: 'His professional skill and reputation gained him many clients whom his winning manners and evenness of temper enabled him to retain as friends.'*

A comparison of two Dorset buildings shows the different stylistic interpretations of the architects to the Victorian revival movement: Ferrey's parsonage house next to the church at Maiden Newton (renamed **Maiden Newton House** sometime after 1938) and The Glebe Farm (recently renamed **Pugin Hall**) at **Rampisham**.

'*The rectorial house stands near the church,*' says Hutchins, '*and is a large ancient building. In the windows are the arms of Wadham, Windham, &c.*'

'*The old parsonage-house was pulled down about 27 years ago, and the present tasteful building, the character of which was suggested by the very picturesque old house, erected on a site further from the river.*'

[Hutchins, 3rd edition, 1863].

Maiden Newton House: the entrance front.

The new rectory at Maiden Newton (*115*) was built to the designs of Ferrey in 1842 for the Reverend the Hon. William Scott who was rector here from 1837–69. The original house was sited within the winter flood plain and probably made damp by the activities of the nearby mill, while the new site was on higher ground with better drainage. Perhaps, as Hutchins infers, the design was suggested by the older house and part of a seventeenth century barn (the present east wing) and doubtless much of the old material was incorporated in the building of it.

The house is L-shaped and built of local dressed stone in bands, with tall elegant Ham stone chimneystacks, arched mullioned windows and dripstones. Its west front has a two-storey Ham stone bay window, also with arched mullions and a plain parapet. The entrance front incorporates an arched porch and another small plain parapet breaks the solid line; this and the horizontal banding in the stonework giving the house, albeit small, a visually grand entrance façade and overall appearance. This charming ensemble however appears almost frivolous by comparison with Pugin's house at Rampisham.

Glebe Farm (*116*) was designed and built between 1845–46 as a rectory for the Reverend F. J. Rooke and his family; he was rector here from 1845 to his death in 1894.[1] Built of local rubble, the rectangular Ham stone windows with mullions and transoms are devoid of decoration and dripstones, the extended eaves over the roof plate shooting rainwater away from the upper storey. Pugin had stated, '...*there should be no features about a building which are not necessary for construction, convenience or propriety,*' and further that, '*all ornament should consist of enrichment of the essential construction of the building*'. Rigidly adhering to his principles, the only decoration and variation here are the dripstone over the arched porch, the curved tracery of the window of the small chapel above, and the larger window that lights the staircase. Here we also find a two-storey bay window, but it is squatly roofed and thereby incorporated into the building, then further tied into it with a protruding string course, which itself is only broken by a chimneybreast on the entrance front. However nothing can detract from the beauty of this house and, as Phoebe Stanton has written, '*It is almost impossible to realise that they* (Pugin's houses) *are of the nineteenth century and are the work of an architect rather than a local mason builder of the fifteenth or sixteenth century.*'

Born at Christchurch, Hampshire, on 1 April 1810, Ferrey was, according to the *Annual National Bibliography*, '...*the youngest son of a gentleman of Huguenot extraction whose family settled in England on the revocation of the Edict of Nantes.*' His father, Benjamin Ferrey senior, was a draper by trade. Brayley notes in *The Antiquities of...Christchurch* that in 1825 he was master of the Leper Hospital of St Mary Magdalen, and in 1840 he was elected Mayor of Christchurch

From his youth Ferrey displayed a love of old buildings and a natural gift for drawing them. By the age of thirteen he had made accurate drawings of the interior of Christchurch Priory and as a pupil at the Grammar School in Wimborne under the tutelage of the Revd James Mayo, spent many hours drawing the Minster church.

He was to become one of the best architectural draughtsmen of the middle period of the nineteenth century; this was partly due to his own natural ability, and to Augustus Charles Pugin (father of Augustus Welby Northmore Pugin) to whom he was sent as a teenage student by his father. Pugin (the elder) was another French Protestant who may well have been known to Ferrey's father; he had also fled from religious persecutions and the French Revolution. An accomplished architectural and topographical illustrator, when first in Britain A. C. Pugin was given employment in the offices of John Nash with whom he collaborated on working drawings for the restoration/rebuilding of the west front of St David's Cathedral, and other projects in Wales. In 1792 he enrolled as a student of the Royal Academy and was later both a publisher and a dealer in antiquarian books relating to architecture and the arts. Ferrey was not only a student of Pugin but also lived with him, his family and other pupils. These included Pugin's son, the comedian Charles Matthews, Joseph Nash and Edward William Cooke, the artists and the architects Talbot Bury, F. T. Dolman and Thomas Larkins Walker.

The actual date that Ferrey was sent to Pugin is not known, possibly during 1824 or 1825. He found the working environment, '*severe and restrictive in the extreme, unrelieved by any of those relaxations essential to the healthy education of youth*'. Relaxation came in the guise of tours which were undertaken both in England and Normandy to visit, draw and measure medieval buildings. The pupils accompanied their master on these tours and Ferrey was later to write, '*the surpassing grandeur of many of the continental churches seems to have thrown him* (Pugin) *quite into raptures*'. In his *Recollections of Pugin* (see below) he writes, '*It was in the month of August, 1825, that, accompanied by some of his pupils, he* (Pugin) *set out for Normandy,...*' He then relates an amusing anecdote of how some pupils distracted Pugin and the Mayor of Jumièges with a constant stream of '*fresh points for discussion*' whilst others made off with an ornamental fragment from a capital that had taken their fancy. The assumption is that he was amongst this group of pupils. From the same work we learn that in July 1826 he accompanied the younger Pugin on a sketching trip to Rochester in Kent. His friendship with A. W. N. Pugin grew; the latter recording in his diary for 21 September 1829 that he, '*Went to Hatfield House with my friend Ferrey to make sketches*'.

A. C. Pugin was the author of numerous books of architectural studies. These resulted directly from the tours and although they were published under his own name, many of the drawings were the work of his pupils. The books were first issued in parts between the years 1828 and 1831, Ferrey contributed 35 signed plates to Pugin and Heath's *Paris and its Environs* and 15 of the 100 plates in *Gothic Ornaments,* bear his signature. *Ornamental Timber Gables,* takes matters further for here the title page of the book states that the plates were '...*drawn on stone by B. Ferrey; under the direction of A. Pugin.*' The master here shows the regard in which he held his pupil, whose work shows great maturity for his eighteen years. The book was published from Pugin's home address, 105, Great Russell Street.

Ferrey soon became steeped in the design and the methods of construction of medieval architects and builders which would influence much of his later Norman and Gothic revival work.

On the death of the elder Pugin in 1832, Ferrey, Walker and A. N. W. Pugin seem to have taken over or were sharing the old Pugin House. In 1833 William Wilkins employed Ferrey for the detailed drawings of the National Gallery and he became more acquainted with the principles of Classical architecture. By 1834 Pugin was in Wiltshire where he was involved in the restoration of the medieval house of John Halle in Salisbury and in the following year the design and construction of his own house at Alderbury. He had effectively left London, and Ferrey and Walker were by June of the same year together in a short-lived partnership, the first volume (in book form) of *Examples of Gothic Architecture*, being jointly published by them '*at their office 105 Great Russell Street.*' This book had had its genesis in 1831 and was originally to be the joint work of the two Pugins but at the time of the elder Pugin's death, only two of the parts issue had been printed. A. Welby Pugin finished the book and he refers to the partnership of Ferrey and Wilkins in a letter written on 31 March 1834 to Edward James Wilson concerning the progress of his work, '...*to compleat the remainder I had a large collection of interesting sketches of domestic architecture taken principally by Myself during the last tour made by my father in the county of somerset, from these I made what I considered the most interesting Selection the delineation of which I entrusted to Messrs. Walker and Ferrey two of My Late Father's most talented pupils for whose zealous cooperation in the compleation of this undertaking I beg to make this public acknowledgement of my thanks.*' Wilson had been a friend of his father's and had supplied the letterpress for some of his publications.

During this period, Ferrey spent some time in and around Christchurch, doubtless often in the company of the younger Pugin who had made his first drawings here at the age of thirteen. Pugin's attempt to purchase a house in the area in 1831 was thwarted by the refusal of his father to act as guarantor, this being around the time of the failure of his first commercial enterprise as a manufacturer of ecclesiastical furniture and carvings. He did however present an altar table to Christchurch Priory in this same year and married his wife, who died in childbirth and was buried in the Priory in 1832. Whether Ferrey and Pugin remained close friends after this period is not known and from the scant references to Ferrey in Pugin's later diaries, it would seem that they did not. Margaret Belcher implies that they may have fallen out or possibly drifted apart over Ferrey's lack of sympathy for Pugin's Catholicism. Pugin's last mention of Ferrey is in a diary entry for 1841.

In 1834, *The Antiquities of the Priory of Christchurch, Hants,* was printed by subscription '*for the Proprietor, Benjamin Ferrey, 105, Great Russell Street, Bloomsbury*'. He drew the views, plans, elevations, sections and details and Edward Wedlake Brayley provided the text. The general consensus of opinion is that in this same year he set up his own architectural practice in London with his offices at the same address, although we know that he had lived at this address for some time previously. The site is now under part of the British Museum.

One of his earliest and most important commissions came in this same year, from Sir George Tapps Gervis, of Hinton Admiral. This was to draw up the plans for the latter's proposed Westover Estate at Bournemouth. Ferrey produced various plans and from these came the Bath Hotel, the Baths, the BelleVue boarding-house, Westover Villas and the Westover Gardens, all designed and built under his direction between 1836 and 1840. Ferrey retained his London address, but probably due to the size of the project, lived in one of the villas for the greater part of it. He seems, from the list of subscribers to his Christchurch enterprise, not to have been a stranger to the local society; Sir George Ivison Tapps (the father of Tapps Gervis) being both subscriber and patron and contributing the engraved plate of the interior of the Countess of Salisbury's Chapel to the work. A. W. N. Pugin is also listed as a subscriber.

He went on from this commission to become one of the most successful architects of the period.

By 1836 Walker's address is given as 106, Great Russell Street on the title page of the second volume of the *Examples*. A street directory of 1838 gives Ferrey's address as 85, Great Russell Street, with Walker still residing at 106.

In 1839 he became a fellow of the Royal Institute of British Architects, an institution of which he was twice Vice-president receiving its Royal Gold Medal in 1870. In 1841 he was appointed Hon. Diocesan Architect of Bath and Wells and in his official capacity superintended much of the restoration of Wells Cathedral. He held this post until his death and through his influential connections and convivial manner received many commissions both in Somerset and Dorset. It is with his works in Dorset that we will later concern ourselves. Another mark of the esteem in which the establishment held him can be seen in the fact that he was the Hon. Secretary of the Committee for the Houses of Parliament after the earlier building's destruction in 1834, where he must once again have come into contact with Pugin.

In 1861 he published his *Recollections of A. N. Welby Pugin, and his Father, Augustus Pugin*. Margaret Belcher, Pugin's bibliographer describes the book as '... *chaotic, unreliable, incomplete, but invaluable*'. The work had apparently been finished some years previously and the delay in publication may have been due in part to the break up of their friendship and to Ferrey's inability to come to terms with Pugin's staunch Catholicism. Ferrey himself almost apologetically describes the nature of his work as being '...*in some popular form a connected sketch of Pugin's career as a professional man, avoiding, where possible, topics which might lead to controversy*'. Here we see a conscious decision to distance himself further from Pugin's Catholicism by assigning Edmund Sheridan Purcell to contribute an appendix to his work in which Pugin's writings and character '...*Are Considered In Their Catholic Aspect*'.

There are no records of their meeting in Dorset despite the ample opportunities for their paths to cross suggesting that there was indeed a rift between them. During 1845–8 Pugin was involved at Rampisham with the design and building of Glebe House, the new school and the restoration of the chancel of the church, for which he also provided the altars, stained glass, font and metal-work. From the scant entries in his diaries we learn that he was first at Rampisham on 15 May, 1845, visiting both Sherbourne (sic) and Lyme where he stayed overnight. Unfortunately, Pugin's diary for 1846 is missing but in 1847 between 29 September and 4 October he visited Dorchester, Milton Abbey, Weymouth, Rampisham and Lyme.[2] His last recorded visit to the area is an overnight stay in Dorchester on 20 September, 1848. During this same period, Ferrey was working relatively close by on the restoration and rebuilding of the churches at Osmington and All Saints, Dorchester; the building of Dorchester Town Hall; the revamping of the west front of Stafford House; and the erection of a new church at Plush. These works would have necessitated the presence of both architects in the county, Pugin having made the additional caveat to his plans for Glebe House that the work was '...*to be executed in a workmanlike & substantial manner to the entire satisfaction of the architect*'.[3]

In 1863 Ferrey was elected a fellow of the Society of Antiquaries. He was also the inventor of a cheap and effective method of stamping plaster, which he patented and made much use of in several of the churches that he built.

In his later life, Ferrey contributed papers to the Institute of Architects and was instrumental in the formation of the Royal Architectural Museum. In October 1877, while he was engaged on the design and erection of a mansion for the Duke of Connaught at Bagshot Park in Surrey, he suffered what appears to have been a stroke which left him with minor paralysis. Although he recovered from the paralysis, he was left with a weak heart and other complimplications and he died peacefully in August 1880. He was buried in Highgate Cemetery in the same grave as his first wife. He was twice married, first in 1836 to Ann, daughter of William Lucas of Stapleton Hall, Stroud Green, Hornsey and secondly in 1872 to Emily, daughter of William Hopkinson. With his first wife, Ferrey had a son and two daughters. The son Edmund Benjamin Ferrey was his pupil and successor in the architectural business.

Footnotes

[1] Pugin's original drawings, estimates and other related papers for The Glebe House are preserved in The Wiltshire Record Office in Trowbridge.

[2] Pugin was possibly consulted about the planned additions to the Roman Catholic Church at Lyme Regis. These were later completed by the architect C. F. Hanson between 1851–52. At Milton Abbey between 1847–48, he made extensive designs for the buildings, decoration and stained glass for Lord Portarlington who was unable to carry out the work due to his inability to collect his rents during the Irish famine. His visits to Sherborne may relate to his later

(unused) designs for the decoration of the choir vault there. These last drawings are now in the Victoria & Albert Museum *(Wedgwood, 1985, 596-607)*.

[3] The quotation ends '... *the contractor finding all labour scaffolding & all new materials specified [signed A Welby Pugin]. NB. The contractor does not provide grates kitchen range or bells.*' Pugin's estimated costs for the work were £1994.10.0. with a deduction of £200 for old materials and in the report of his original survey, made on 15 May, after describing the building as, '... *so dilapidated as to be unfit for repair...*' states, '*portions of the roof & floor timbers flooring boards, framed doors plates, and walling stones are available for the new building.*'

THE DORSET BUILDINGS OF BENJAMIN FERREY

Tarrant Hinton Rectory *(117)* built in Ferrey's best Tudor style, is a tall red-brick building with blue headers and stone dressings. The Royal Commission dates the house to c. 1850 but Newman and Pevsner give it a date of 1836, their information coming from the Revd. G. Sealy. In 1874 he rebuilt the chancel of the church here *(118)*. At **Compton Valance** in 1839–40 Ferrey rebuilt the main body of the church and the Parsonage House, the latter now hidden away behind trees to the south-west of the church. The church is built in the thirteenth century Decorated style of architecture and has a polygonal apse *(118)*.

It was while working on the rebuilding of the church here that Ferrey met Arthur Acland (1811–57) who was both architect and stonemason. Acland latterly worked with Ferrey on many occasions and was Clerk of the Works on three of Ferrey's Dorset projects; Dorchester Hospital in the same year, All Saints church in Dorchester, and the church at Little Bredy. He was the artist responsible for the carvings on the west door and the stops on the hood-moulds of the windows at All Saints, and at Little Bredy in 1850. He may well have been responsible for the carving here.

Dorchester: All Saints.

Clyffe House at Tincleton is a full Tudor revival house of brown Broadmayne brick with Portland stone dressings, built in 1842 for Charles Porcher. It is E-shaped on the entrance front, with gables and large mullioned and transomed windows throughout, most with curved lights and hood-moulds in the best Dorset tradition. The photograph is of the south face *(119)*. Although there is no documentary evidence, on stylistic grounds the schoolhouse here must be attributable to Ferrey too. He also built the school at Buckland Newton, but more recent work has obscured the original design.

Between 1843 and 1848 Ferrey worked on the churches of **All Saints** in Dorchester, rebuilt in the full Decorated style with a

stone spire between 1843–1845. He rebuilt the nave, aisle and transepts of **Winterborne Whitechurch** in 1844 *(120)* and between 1845–6 built the church at **Melplash**. This is a full blown Norman building, with a central crossing tower, apsidal chancel and transepts, the north transept with its own smaller apsidal end *(121)* Ferrey built the church for James Bandinel, whose father had been Vicar of Netherbury. At **Osmington** *(120)*, Ferrey rebuilt all but the tower of the church in the Perpendicular style in 1846 *(86);* at **Plush** in 1848 another, smaller, building in the Perpendicular style with a bellcote *(122)*.

This last one is a personal favourite, the secluded situation, partly obscured by trees adding somehow to the compactness of the design. In all of these church buildings, whilst doubtless observing the wishes of his clients, he has taken, once again, a slightly independent stand against the rigid conformity of Pugin's ideas.

In the same year that he was working at Plush, Ferrey received another commission from John Floyer of **Stafford House**. Floyer had purchased the house in 1830 and the previous owner, Nicholas Gould, had consulted Humphrey Repton on what improvements could be made to the north-west front of the house. Repton published his ideas in 1816 in his *Fragments on the Theory and Practice of Landscape Gardening*. The old house of 1633, was only a single room deep with some remains of earlier buildings at the back. An eighteenth century drawing in the house shows it prior to the new building. Conjecture as to the name of the architect who carried out the work here was settled when Ferrey's office stamp was found on one of the original architect's drawings. He faithfully carried out the work to the original designs of Repton and in keeping with the style of the original house, the same pale grey limestone and rubble with ashlar dressings and Purbeck stone tiles for the roof. The windows, too, are in keeping, albeit of different, larger, proportions. The front is symmetrical except for the two-tier bay window on the gabled end. The recessed entrance with two open bays between two blind bays, the latter containing niches, is itself reminiscent of the entrance at Warmwell, but here the front has the feel of a loggia *(123)*.

Also between 1847–48 Ferrey built the **Town Hall** in **Dorchester** *(124)*1 above the Corn Exchange. Built of Broadmayne brick with Bath stone dressings, this is again in the Tudor style with a two-storey oriel window on the east front. The angled clock tower was added, by Ferrey, in 1864 and the portal added in 1876.

In 1850, Ferrey almost entirely rebuilt the church at **Little Bredy** (with the exception of the tower on which he placed a recessed spire) in the Decorated style *(124)*. The fenestration is all his save for the small original Decorated window in the tower and the chancel lancets. He also made additions to Bridehead.

The chancel of **Frampton** church was rebuilt to Ferrey's design in 1862 *(125)* and has some exquisite carvings to the stops of the

window labels by Benjamin Grassby, especially the head of Christ with a crown of thorns. Ferrey's design was given high praise in the *Dorchester County Chronicle* where the re-opening of the chancel, '*...formerly of a very debased character, but now is a gem of architecture after beautiful designs by Benjamin Ferret ....*' is reported in the issue of 7 August 1862.

In 1863 Ferrey was responsible for the restoratioin and rebuilding of Long Bredy church. The stone carving was again by Grassby.

Ferrey's last commission in Dorset would appear to have been the building of the church of Holy Trinity in Dorchester between 1875 and 1876.

He also designed and built the rectory at Cattistock, which has been subsequently altered making the original work difficult to recognise, and in 1839, the old Dorchester County Hospital, in Princes Street, which at the time of writing is undergoing redevelopment.

Three label stops.

Frampton.

Compton Valance.

Frampton.

SHOP FRONTS

The oldest shop front in the county is probably the Tudor example on the half-timbered range of buildings opposite the tower of the church in **Cerne Abbas**. The buildings date from c.1500 and the carved spandrels of the fenestration here would seem to suggest a shop front. The end cottage of the eighteenth century range in **Puddletown** *(126)* (one of which is dated 1772) had the first-floor bay-window added before the end of that century and in the early years of the next a shop-window was inserted in the south front; alas, with the inexorable rise of the out of-town-supermarket, as in so many other small villages, the shop has closed and the building reverted to a dwelling house.

The county still has a goodly number of late eighteenth century and early nineteenth century shop-fronts but for me the finest example is in East Street, **Bridport** *(127)*. This is a good example of how buildings change with use. East Street is part of the main thoroughfare of a busy market town and until recent years (and probably for the same reason as above) buildings like this were at a premium. Originally built in the seventeenth century as the George Inn, it was refaced in the late eighteenth century when the elegant bow-windows were inserted on the façade, then in the nineteenth century the scrolled fascia-board was added.

Cerne Abbas: former shop front.

Hampshire and Dorset, and from this the Branksome estate (as it developed) took its name. The gates to this house opening on to the Poole road received the appellation 'County Gates', which name has survived and fallen into common use. Westbourne in 1876 consisted of the small Alum Cliff estate, the beginnings of Alumhurst Road and Alum Chine Road, and the Westborne Hotel. The railway and the opening of West Station fuelled the development of this suburb (of Poole) and by 1885 Henry Joy had designed and built the **Westbourne Arcade**. He had built the Criterion Arcade in the centre of Bournemouth eighteen years before and the design of both is similar. Symmetrical brick façades, with stone dressings can be seen at either end *(128)*, the two blocks ending with four shops facing the street, each of three bays with pointed gables over the two inner bays, these bays curved inwards to the arched entrances. Above the arcade is a glass tunnel-vault and on the inner faces of the entrance façades over the windows, Joy's name and the date of the construction are proudly displayed *(128)*. The fascia-boards of many of the shops may have been altered but most remain as built. Look above the pure commercial level and between the ironwork, rainwater heads, pipes, wires and paraphernalia, and see the faces of the corbels that support the vaulting leering querulously back at you. A joy in themselves.

The expansion of **Bournemouth** after its initial beginnings in 1836 was quite slow but by 1876 it had reached its own prescribed boundaries and the adjacent suburbs of Springbourne and Boscombe to the east were swallowed up. To the west of the town, as early as 1855 a Mr Packe built himself a house, Branksome Tower, just west of the county boundary between

Iwerne Minster has a purpose-built butcher's shop *(129)* dating from the 1920s, the quaint painted sign (although not the painting) and the interior tiling all being part of Ismay's model village. Happily there is still a village butcher plying his trade here and long may he continue!

TWO CHURCHYARD MONUMENTS

While we were setting up the shot of **Osmington** church and as usual, waiting for the sun, we realised that we had placed the camera tripod next to an interesting gravestone. It commemorates the death of 'Henry Baily, who departed this life the 20th of September, 1774. Aged 34' *(130)*. The carved panel above depicts a boy on the Day of Judgement, breaking free from a table tomb, in response to the trumpet call from above, the Archangel's trumpet sticking out from the clouds at the top left of the tombstone. The head of the tomb is broken and the boy is in the action of throwing off his shroud and the heavy stone slab with which the tomb was sealed. The top and sides of the stone have a carved ribbon border. Further investigation revealed another gravestone of the same date south-east of the chancel.

These depict two cherubs either side of a mourning figure, about to place a crown on its head, while holding in their other hands a scroll that reads 'Be thou faithful unto death and I will give thee a crown of life.' These two gravestones were carved by the same unknown hand and other examples of this carver's work can be found at Portland. The work is vigorous and unsophisticated for the late eighteenth century and owes more to early medieval carvers than to other more contemporary styles, but this does not detract from their obvious charm.

The trihedron monument to the Revd Thomas Rackett in the churchyard at **Spetisbury** *(130)* is better known. Rackett died in 1808 and the monument is signed '*Marshall of Blandford*'.

BEAMINSTER CHURCH

The church of St Mary (*131*) is a good example of the way in which the architecture and subsequent appearance of a building, all or parts therof (this note refers mainly to the west tower), has been altered over time.

John Leland tells us, '*Bemistre is a praty market town in Dorsetshire, and usith much housbandry, and lyith in one streat from north to south: and in a nother from west to est. Ther is a fair chappelle of ease in this town. Netherby is the parish church to it: and Bemistre is a prebend to the chirch of Saresbyri*'. Both Netherbury and Beaminster were in St Osmund's gift to the church of Salisbury in 1091. Unfortunately there is no mention of any actual church buildings at either place. The bowl of the font and a small piece of re-used moulding with dog-tooth ornament in the staircase of the rood loft offer evidence of a Norman building.

We know from the register of Simon de Gandavo, Bishop of Salisbury, that there was a church dedicated to the Virgin Mary here in the late thirteenth century and in a letter to the Dean of Salisbury dated 16 December 1298, de Gandavo expressed his concern that some of the appropriated churches in the Archdeaconry of Dorset were at that time unconsecrated! In a further letter of 1303 the bishop wrote of his surprise that despite his concerns of some four years earlier many of the buildings (including Netherbury and Meaminsuter) were still unconsecrated. He also made clear his intention to set matters right himself and from his itinerary we know that he visited Beaminster in October of the same year. This building was cruciform in plan with a central tower, nave, chancel and transpets.

In the late fifteenth and sixteenth centuries the building was again enlarged by the addition of of side aisles, the removal of the central tower and the erection of the magnificent west tower with its small annexe to the south-west. This progression is well recorded in Pitfield's *Dorset Parish Churches* (1981).

The photograph (*9*) shows the west front of this 'new' tower with its wealth of decoration, crocketted pinnacles and figure sculpture. Justly described as 'one of the glories of the west country' the elegance and flamboyant style echo the school of tower builders in nearby Somerset.

But here all is not what it first appears to be for this early sixteenth century tower has suffered many restorations and affronts to its fabric over the last five centuries. Hutchins tells us, '*In 1503 a legacy was given towards the building of a new tower here*'. There is no evidence of any such legacy and this statement could be the misinterpretation of one of the terms of the will of William Mason, dated 10 February, 1503/4 in which he gave instructions that his body was to be '*buried under the new tower*'. All that can be deduced from this is that the main work of the tower was completed at that date. Beaminster residents of the next century or so would have seen roughly what we see today, but Hutchins in the second edition of his history (1796) wrote of the 38 pinnacles that decorate the tower that '*those on the top were entirely destroyed at the Reformation, or during the Civil War, and age has made great havock with the rest*'. And that '*On the west and north sides are many empty niches*' and despite records that, '*The Church and Tower were much repaired*' in 1659; and that in 1667 Hugh Sugar was paid '*2s 6d.*' for '*...5 clamps for ye pinnacles at the toope of ye towre*' and a further '*4s. 00d*' to Henry Peach '*...for stownes & 2 days labor about the pinicles of the towre & Lyme.*' (Hine, 1914) The engraving printed in the letterpress depicts the tower without pinnacles on the parapet. This same engraving also shows that although the opening of the great west window has remained the same, the fenestration was altered and replaced in the restoration of 1877–78. During these restorations two of the original finials from the demolished pinnacles were discovered embedded in modern work on the roof of the tower and these served as models for the new ones which were carved by Mr C. Trask of Stoke-sub-Hamdon in Ham hill stone; also at this time Harry Hems of Exeter carved six new figures to fill those niches that were despoiled at the Reformation. These replacements gave back to the tower the elegance that the original builders had intended and which had been lost for some two hundred years.

MODERN ARCHITECTURE OF DORSET

Portland Lighthouse *(132)* was built in 1905 and supersedes those built c.1867. Although not an ugly building it cannot strictly be termed beautiful. But what a stunning photograph.

Bournemouth, Poole and **Dorchester** have some noteworthy modern buildings. The buildings of Bournemouth and Poole are, all but the first, office buildings and those at Dorchester are from the Poundbury development of the Duchy of Cornwall.

The San Remo Towers, the Italianate block of flats near Boscombe Chine, built between 1936 and 1938, by Hector O. Hamilton of Hamilton & Green *(133)* would be more at home in Los Angeles or some other American City, yet here it is in Dorset. The tiled door and window surrounds and other smaller features, such as the detailing of the gates into the central courtyard reinforce the Continental feeling. Beneath this inner courtyard, the building incorporates a car park, one of the first so to do.

Described by some as horrendous, others have always been drawn to it, and whilst it cannot really be described as beautiful, it has a charm and uniqueness that at least inspire and draw comment from all who see it.

Bournemouth: San Remo Towers.

The rectangular **Abbey Life** building of 1976 *(134)*, by Leslie Jones & Partners partly resembles the bridge of an ocean liner, the floors and suites of offices piled neatly up to the granary-like tower in the centre. At night, when illuminated, it further takes on the look of an ocean liner.

Not far from this is the **MacCarthy & Stone** building *(135)*, designed by the Hendy Green Partnership in 1987. The shape, along with the smoked glass windows with their glazing bars,

makes the façade look like the hessian on a 1930s radio. Another masterpiece.

The **Zurich** building *(136)* on Richmond Hill in Bournemouth and the **Merck** building in Poole *(136)* are both giant glass reflectors, the first an alien craft that has landed amongst us, lost contact with the mother ship and sits quietly awaiting rescue.

Barclays Bank in Poole *(137)* is designed as an enormous letter B, but the photograph has been taken from the adjacent car park, which gives it the appearance of a medieval castle. The lower stages of the walls jutting slightly out and the tops of the tall pilaster-like piers of the building, take the form of battlements from which large stones and other objects could be dropped and projected at the approaching enemy; or perhaps in this modern age to slow down the progress of those requiring an overdraft?

Another interesting new design is the round tower-like building near Blandford *(138)*, with its central chimneystack, a cross between Umbrella cottage and a medieval church with its nave and chancel behind.

The Work of the Duchy of Cornwall in Dorchester *(139)* seeks to combine some of the better elements of Dorset architecture from preceding centuries and give them a modern interpretation, but I cannot help feeling that many of the buildings have a French or continental flavour to them. This is especially true of the Brownsword market building *(140)*, with its columned ground floor, angled buttresses and the steep pitch of the gabled roof. Here is a building similar to what might have been erected by the builders of medieval bastides, or perhaps even the Normans who conquered us nearly one thousand years ago. Perhaps architecture has turned full circle?

THE PHOTOGRAPHS

Portland: Bow and Arrow Castle.

Christchurch Priory.

Corfe Castle in a mist.

Owermoigne: Moigne Court.

Afflington: the Manor House.

Kingston: Scoles Manor.

Church Knowle: Barnston Manor.

Wimborne Minster: St Cuthberga.

Studland: St Nicholas, the interior.

Studland: St Nicholas, the north elevation.

St Aldhelm's Head: the Chapel.

Winterborne Thomson: St Andrew.

Forde Abbey.

Woodsford Castle.

Abbotsbury: the tithe barn and fishpond.

Abbotsbury: St Catherine's Chapel.

Purse Caundle: the Manor House, south front.

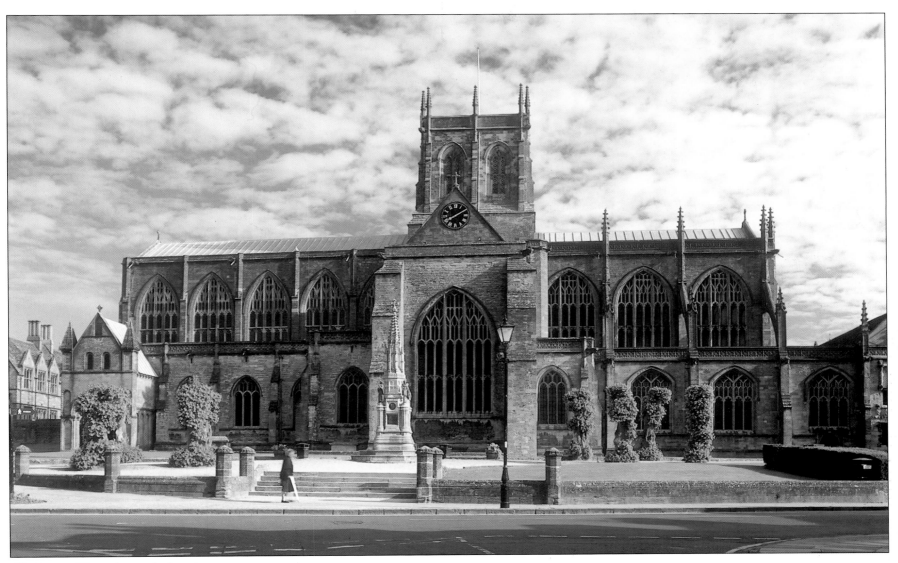

Sherborne Abbey: the south elevation.

Sherborne: almshouses.

Athelhampton Hall: the west wing and oriel window.

Athelhampton Hall: the garden front.

Athelhampton Hall: the dovecote.

Sandford Orcas: the Manor House.

Beaminster: Parnham, the entrance front.

Beaminster: Parnham, the south front.

Charminster: Wolfeton House.

Charminster: the Riding House.

Wimborne St Giles: the Riding House.

Trent: the Chantry.

Winterborne Clenston: the Manor House.

Edmondsham House: the north-west elevation.

Creech Grange: the Georgian façade.

Melplash: Melplash Court.

Hanford House: the entrance front.

Hanford House: the east front.

Warmwell: Warmwell House.

Pamphill: Court Cottage.

Chantmarle: the entrance front.

Chantmarle: the rear view.

Puncknowle: the Manor House.

Creech Grange: the entrance front.

Over Compton: Compton House.

Iwerne Minster: The Oak House.

East Lulworth: Lulworth Castle.

East Lulworth: St Mary (R. C.)

East Lulworth: the North Lodges

East Lulworth: the Wareham road lodge.

Bindon Abbey: Abbey House.

Chideock: Roman Catholic chapel of Our Lady of Martyrs and St Ignatius.

79

Anderson Manor.

Wool: Woolbridge Manor House.

Waterston House: the south front.

Waterston House: the east front.

West Stafford: Stafford House, the east front.

Hamoon: Hamoon House.

Mapperton House.

Pamphill: High Hall.

Chettle: Chettle House.

Chettle: granary on staddle stones.

Horton: St Wolfreda.

Horton: Horton Tower.

Woodlands: the Round House.

Blandford Forum: the Old House.

Blandford Forum: the Town Hall.

Blandford Forum: The Old Greyhound Inn.

*Weymouth: end of terrace
in St Mary Street.*

Encombe House.

Iwerne Courtney: Ranston.

Winterborne Came: Came House.

Smedmore House: north front.

Kimmeridge: Clavel Tower.

Portland: St George Reforne.

Poole: Congregational Chapel, Skinner Street.

Stanbridge: Cottage Orné

Lyme Regis: Umbrella Cottage.

Chantmarle: lodge houses.

Lyme Regis: Madiera Cottages.

Edmondsham: the Old Rectory.

Kingston Lacy.

Puddletown: the Old Manor.

Chalmington: Stable Manor.

Moreton: St Nicholas.

Milton Abbas: Milton Abbey.

Pulham: the Rectory.

Christchurch: Highcliffe Castle.

Christchurch: Highcliffe Castle,
the entrance porch.

111

Winterborne Clenston: St Nicholas.

Winterborne Clenston: trophy of arms.

112

Monkton Wyld Court: the entrance front.

Monkton Wyld Court: the garden front.

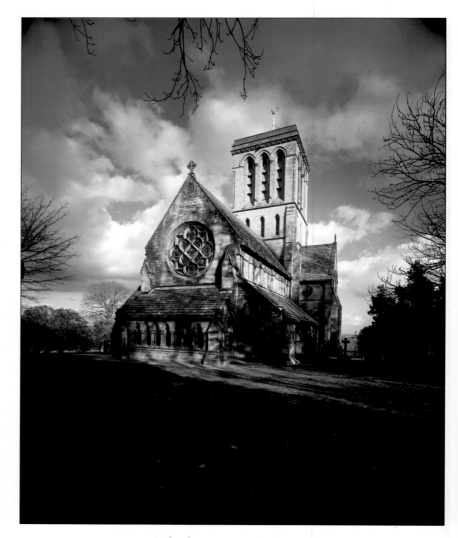

Kingston: St James. The east and west ends.

Maiden Newton: Maiden Newton House, the garden front.

Rampisham: Pugin Hall.

Tarrant Hinton: the Old Rectory.

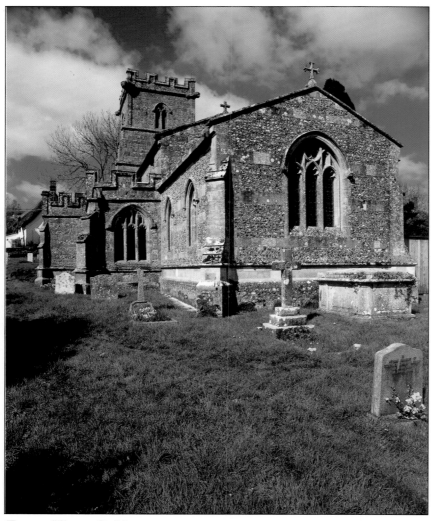

Tarrant Hinton: St Mary.

Compton Valance: St Thomas of Canterbury.

Tincleton: Clyffe House.

Winterborne Whitechurch: St Mary.

Osmington: St Osmund.

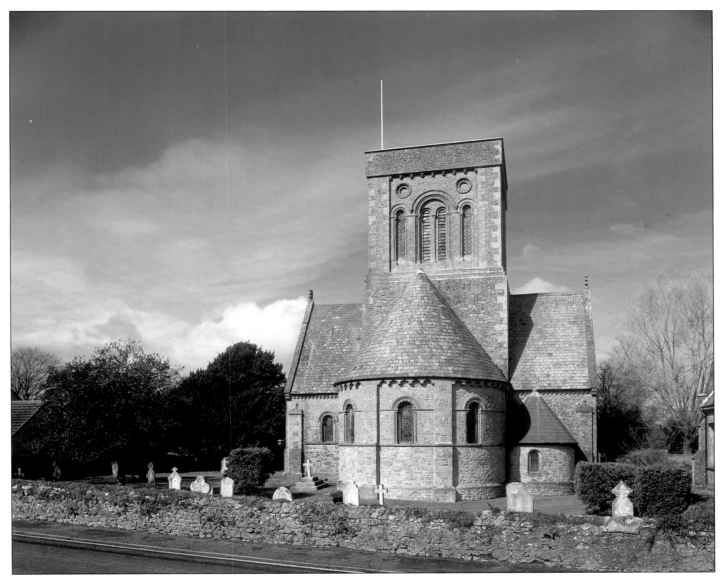

Melplash: Christ Church.

Plush: St John Baptist.

West Stafford: Stafford House, the west front.

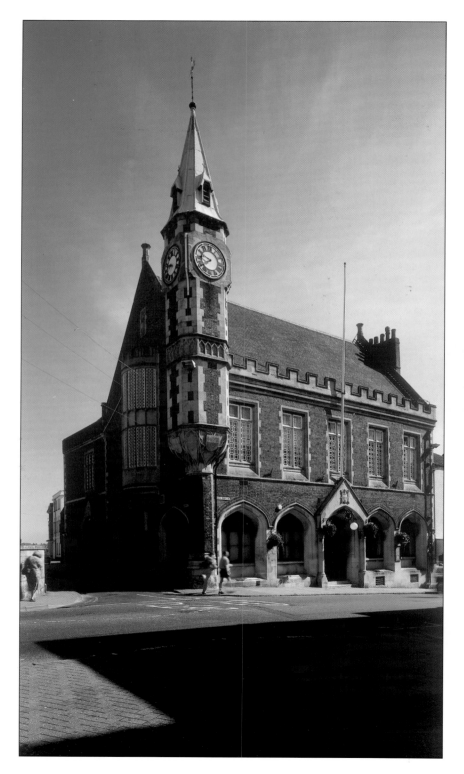

Little Bredy: St Michael.

Dorchester: the Town Hall.

124

Frampton: St Mary.

Puddletown: former shop.

Bridport: shop front in East Street.

Bournemouth: Westbourne Arcade, exterior and interior.

Iwerne Minster: butcher's shop.

Osmington: Baily monument.

Spetisbury: Rackett monument.

Beaminster: St Mary.

Portland: Lighthouse.

Bournemouth: San Remo Towers.

Bournemouth: Abbey Life building.

Bournemouth: MacCarthy and Stone building.

Bournemouth: Zurich building.

Poole: Merck building.

Poole: Barclays Bank building.

Blandford: tower house.

Dorchester: Poundbury.

Dorchester: Brownsword market building.

GLOSSARY

Aisle: open space on one or both sides of a central space, in a church, the aisles are divided from the nave by piers or columns, usually with arches.

Apse: vaulted semicircular (or polygonal) end to the chancel of a church or chapel.

Architrave: in classical architecture, the lowest member of the Entablature (q. v.) which rests on the capitals of the supporting columns.

Ashlar: accurately squared stones with a smooth face, used for masonry walling, where it is laid in regular courses with fine joints, and for quoins and other detailing.

Bailey: a term used to describe the outer wall of a medieval castle or keep. Later the term was applied to internal courts of the castle, e.g. the inner bailey, outer bailey, etc.

Bays: internal divisions of a building, made with solid walls, ceiling beams, etc., on the exterior of the building the division into bays is by the fenestration.

Cartouche: ornately framed tablet usually with an inscription.

Censer: vessel in which incense is burnt.

Chancel: the east end of a church in which the principal altar is placed.

Cinquefoil: see *Foil*.

Clerestory or Clearstorey: the upper storey of the nave walls of a church, pierced by windows to illuminate the interior of the church-this fact explaining the word 'clear.'

Clustered pillar or column: an apparently single column composed of a number of pillars of stone shafts attached to each other.

Corinthian: see *Order*.

Cornice: in classical architecture, the uppermost section of the entablature, but in more general use to describe the projecting decorative feature on the top of a wall, arch, etc.

Curtain wall: the exterior wall of a castle, the sections of that wall between the towers.

Cusp: in mediaeval architecture, a projection carved on the underside of an arch, dividing the arch into a series of 'foils.' (q. v.)

Diapered brickwork: surface decoration composed of patterns in the brickwork, squares, lozenges, etc.,

Doric: see *Order*.

Enciente (Fr.): the wall surrounding a castle or fort, more properly a form of enclosure.

Entablature: in classical architecture the arrangement of the architrave, frieze and cornice, above the supporting columns in any of the classical orders.

Fenestration: the arrangement of the windows on the façade of a building.

Flying buttress: a stone buttress in the form of an arched prop, the arch transmitting the weight and thrust of a vault or roof away from the main wall of the building to a supporting pier.

Foil: a small single arc between the cusps of tracery or an arch. In tracery the circular formations of the foils are expressed as trefoil, quatrefoil, cinquefoil and multifoil.

Hall: originally the principal room of a medieval house wherein the occupants lived, fed and slept, in later times, the principal dwelling in a rural area.

Herring-bone: brick, stone, tile or other building material laid diagonally, opposing courses laying in opposite directions to form a zig zag pattern on the face of a wall.

Hood-mould: also called a dripstone or label. A projecting moulding over a lintel, arch, window arch, etc., to throw off water. They are often terminated with carved heads or ornamental shields.

Hipped Roof: roof where the normally vertical ends are sloped.

Ionic: see *Order*.

Jamb: straight side of an archway, doorway, or window.

Keep: the central or inner tower of a mediaeval castle.

Lancet: slender window with a pointed arch.

Machicolations: a series of galleried openings raised on brackets on the outside of a castle tower or wall behind the embattled parapet of a mediaeval castle through which boiling liquid or missiles could be dropped on to the heads of assailants. They were introduced to Western Europe after the Crusades, the lower courses of towers are sometimes splayed outwards to add horizontal force to any missiles dropped.

Modillion: small bracket supporting a cornice. In mediaeval architecture often carved with human or animal heads, floral decoration, shields, etc.,

Motte (Fr.): artificial mound of earth fortified as a castle, the earliest examples with a timber stockade around the top; later with a stone 'Keep' (q. v.)

Mullion: vertical bar of stone or wood dividing a window into 'lights.'

Nave: the main body of the church often with aisles and transepts.

Niche: ornamental wall recess, normally with an arched top, usually designed to hold a statue or urn, but often as an open decorative feature.

Order: In classical architecture a column with base, shaft, capital and entablature in one of the following styles: Corinthian, Doric, Ionic and Tuscan. Within these four styles there exist many variations and a specialist architectural dictionary should be consulted for further clarification.

Oriel: a form of bay-window projecting from the wall face of the upper storey of a building, supported on brackets or corbelling.

Pediment: triangular low pitched gable above a portico and above doors and windows. A broken pediment is one where the centre of the base is left open and an open pediment is one where the sloping sides are left open at the apex of the triangle.

Pilasters: shallow piers attached to a wall.

Piscina (originally from the Lat. Piscis, a fish): originally a pond or basin for fish. In Christian churches, a basin with a drain for washing the communion vessels, usually set in a niche to the south of the altar.

Plat Bands: a flat rectangular moulding.

Quatrefoil: see *Foil*.

Relieving Arch: an arch of brick or stone (usually hidden) built over a lintel or opening to relieve it from some of the pressure created by the brick or stone of the walling above.

Roof plate: horizontal timber or stone framing to support the timbers of the roof.

Rubble: building stone, neither regular or worked, which is therefore impossible to lay in regular courses.

Sarcophagus: carved coffin

Solar: in early mediaeval houses, the upper living-room, in later medieval and Tudor houses, a sitting-room or parlour for the owner's family away from the communal life of the hall.

Spandrel: the triangular space between the outer curves of an arch.

String course: projecting horizontal band of moulding, stone or brick, running across the face of a building.

Tracery: The intersecting ribwork in the upper part of a window.

Transept: the transverse arms of a cruciform church, normally aligned north and south.

Transom: horizontal bar of stone or wood across a mullioned window.

Trefoil: see *Foil*.

Tuscan: see *Order*.

Undercroft: a range of vaulted store-rooms in a medieval building beneath the principal room or rooms.

BIBLIOGRAPHY

Belcher, M. *A. W. N. Pugin. An annotated critical bibliography.* 1987.

Belcher, M. *The Collected Letters of A.W.N. Pugin.* Volume 1 1830-1842. Oxford, 2001.

Bell, N. & A. G. *From Harbour to Harbour. The Story of Christchurch, Bournemouth, and Poole from the Earliest Times to the Present Day.* By Mrs. Arthur Bell. With Twelve Full-page Illustrations by Arthur G. Bell. 1916.

Chafin, W. *Anecdotes and History of Cranborne Chase.* Introduction by Desmond Hawkins. Stanbridge, 1991. (A reprint of the first edition of 1881.)

Eedle, Marie de G. *A History of Beaminster.* Chichester, 1984.

Fägersten, A. T*he Place-Names of Dorset.* Uppsala, 1933.

Hardy, W. M. *Old Swanage. Or Purbeck Past and Present.* New and Revised Edition with Three Supplementary Chapters. Dorchester, 1910.

Heath, S. & Prideaux, W. de C. *Some Dorset Manor Houses.* Derby & London, 1907.

Hutchins, J. *The History and Antiquities of the County of Dorset.* Third Edition, 1861-1870.

Hyland, P. *Purbeck. The Ingrained Island.* 1978.

Legg, R. *Purbeck Island. The industrial, social and natural history of a corner of England.* Revised edition, Wincanton, 1989.

Machin, R. 'Barnston Manor, Dorset, and Aydon Castle, Northumberland: A Re-assessment of Two Late Thirteenth-Century Houses.' *Archaeological Journal,* 134 (1977), 297-302.

Mills, A. D. *The Place-Names of Dorset.* 3 volumes, 1977-1989.

Newman, J. & Pevsner, N. *The Buildings of England: Dorset.* Harmondsworth, 1972.

Oswald, A. *Country Houses of Dorset.* Second, revised and enlarged edition, 1959. [Reprinted, Tiverton, 1994.]

Pitfield, F. P. *Dorset Parish Churches A-D.* Milborne Port, 1981.

Proceedings of the Dorset Natural History & Archaeological Society. 1876-date.

Renn, D. *Norman Castles in Britain.* Second edition, 1973.

Royal Commission on Historical Monuments-Dorset. 1952-1975.

Wake-Smart, T. W. *A Chronicle of Cranborne and The Cranborne Chase.* Second edition with an Introduction by Desmond Hawkins. Stanbridge, 1983. [First published 1841.]

Warne, C. *Ancient Dorset.* Bournemouth, 1872.

Wedgewood, A. *A. W. N. Pugin and the Pugin Family.* Catalogues of Architectural Drawings in the Victoria and Albert Museum. 1985.

Wood, M. E. *Thirteenth-Century Domestic Architecture in England. 1950.* Supplement to the *Archaeological Journal* volume CV.

Wood, M. E. *The English Mediaeval House.* 1965.

Scoles Manor: the hall window.